Managing Uncertainty and Change in Social Work and Social Care

Ken Johnson
and
Isabel Williams

Russell House Publishing

Published in 2007 by:
Russell House Publishing Ltd.
4 St. George's House
Uplyme Road
Lyme Regis
Dorset DT7 3LS

Tel: 01297-443948
Fax: 01297-442722
e-mail: help@russellhouse.co.uk
www.russellhouse.co.uk

British Library Cataloguing-in-publication Data:
A catalogue record for this book is available from the British Library.

ISBN: 978-1-905541-07-2

Typeset by TW Typesetting, Plymouth, Devon
Printed by Biddles Ltd, King's Lynn

Contents

About the authors

Ken Johnson and Isabel Williams are Senior Lecturers within the Social Work and Social Care Department, Institute of Health and Social Care, Anglia Ruskin University.

They have social work and management qualifications and have worked for many years within the public sector and social care settings at both practitioner and manager levels.

Isabel Williams BA (Hons.) 1st, DipSW, Master in Business Administration, PGCE

Ken Johnson CQSW, Cert. Counselling, Dip. Counselling, PGCE, Cert. Public Relations, Dip. Management.

Acknowledgements

Both Ken and Isabel would like to thank their families as well as members of the Social Work and Social Care Department, Anglia Ruskin University, for their continued encouragement. The list is endless but, specifically, mention must be made of Clare Seymour and Maire Maisch for their support.

Of particular note, they would both like to thank Dr Greg Mantle, Reader in Advanced Practice and Research for the hours he devoted to proof reading, support and guidance.

Isabel and Ken would also like to thank their social work students who have been the voice of reality in practice throughout.

Introduction

This book confronts the uncertain reality of contemporary social work practice and management. We live and work within the context of uncertainty brought about by external changes that have an impact at individual and team level, driven by events occurring in the wider organisation or as a result of legislation, policy or differing demands which appear many miles away from practice. The effects have both a direct and an indirect impact on all aspects of an organisation, the teams, its service users, staff, their roles and the general culture and morale. Such change disrupts the established equilibrium and normally it is the social work manager who has to interpret and disseminate the effects of change to others in a way that is understandable and practicable. Being able to cope with a changing environment is a skill and requirement that all social workers need to be able to understand regardless of their role or location – be it within a statutory setting, a community based setting, a multi-professional team, or even as an independent consultant or someone who is part of a virtual team.

We believe that social work practitioners and first line managers are poorly equipped with the tools and strategies needed to deal adequately with the changing environment in which they work. There is no doubt that social work practitioners and managers have a difficult and complex role and are sometimes caught in the middle of competing pressures from their team members, the organisation, the external community and the wider changing environment. This is even more apparent as social workers rise within the echelons of the organisation and consequently take on more responsibilities and more difficult expectations of the various stakeholders they need to satisfy.

While the specialist nature of the professional task is well established, this book will question the historical separation of practice and management functions. It will be of significant benefit to social work students, as an introduction to the realities of practice, as well as practitioners and first time managers who grapple with the challenges and demands of service delivery. While there are numerous textbooks on management, this book specifically focuses on managing the uncertainty caused by changing environments. It combines practice and theory through a textbook approach accompanied by dialogue and discussion. Numerous activities and exercises will bring to life the art and science of management of uncertainty for the individual social worker and social care manager and bridges the gap between the practice and management functions. It will allow the practitioner and manager to use strategies, traditionally regarded as the province of management, in order to enhance their role.

To manage change and the consequent uncertainty effectively, practitioners and managers need to understand the external world, how this impacts on organisations and how this then impacts on their teams and on them as individuals. Indeed, this is identified by the Quality Assurance Agency social work benchmark statement 2.23 which makes it clear that all social workers need to have a contextual understanding of their work:

> *Social work, both as an occupational practice and as an academic subject, evolves, adapts and changes in response to social, political and economic challenges and demands of contemporary social welfare policy, practice and legislation.*

(Quality Assurance Agency, 2000: 11)

Through an Audit Commission overview of joint reviews undertaken between 1996 and 2003, Mead (2004: 49) states that what works best is a business-like approach underpinned by the values of social care. The report argues that the top performing councils share similar characteristics:

- See good social services as central to building inclusive, stronger communities.
- Have a synergy about the vision and direction of social care across political, corporate and service levels.
- Have a clear, articulated sense of direction coming from the top, that is well informed by users and frontline views.
- Are obsessed by what is being delivered at the frontline.
- Emphasise the whole network of care and support, and focus less on diverse boundaries.
- Have an informed, Best Value approach to service development and no 'sacred cows' about how or what services should be provided by whom.
- Ensure the basics work well: understand and manage risk, are clear about priorities, comply with statutory regulatory requirements.
- Manage the performance of people, activity, costs and outcomes fairly using a range of techniques.
- Put a high premium on supporting and developing staff.
- Convey a culture of enthusiasm, team working and eagerness to improve.

Mead's findings provide a useful summary of the characteristics and attributes that constitute successful local authorities. One is left to wonder, however, how the attributes of these successful authorities can be replicated in other public organisations, some of whom are facing a climate of retrenchment. It also presupposes that the structure for delivery of social care services will remain within local authority and health care as the main providers. It is interesting to note, for example, that the Audit Commission Corporate Discussion Paper *Assessment of Local Services beyond 2008* (August 2006) makes reference to a 'greater variety in organisational structures' (point 16) less regulation and 'the need for a more devolved approach, where local people have more powers and resources to influence the key decisions which affect their community' (point 14). We will expand on these thoughts in Chapter 8.

The structure of the book

There are eight chapters that follow a coherent and logical process of looking at the impact of change in different contexts of practice and draw from the Audit Commission report. Each chapter first considers the macro drivers of change within the given context and then clearly and simply relates these to practice opportunities and challenges. The chapters are interweaved with exercises that can be completed within a group, team, organisation or classroom setting, or as individual reference points.

Chapter 1: The Challenges of Change

This chapter will begin by setting the scene and identifying the drivers of change from the external environment. A STEEP model will be introduced as a way of highlighting the challenges – societal, technological, environmental, economic and political. We will introduce the reader to concepts such as supply and demand as a precursor to resources and budget decision-making; we will consider the changing demographic environment and how this impacts on the social work role; we will consider joined up working and the changing culture of practice. This chapter will then consider how the individual practitioner manager and their team can work with and alongside change without feeling threatened, disempowered or deskilled. Activities, exercises and diagrams will be introduced throughout the chapter to guide the reader from general to specific ways of considering change and the impact of change on themselves as practitioners, professionals and managers. We consider what we mean by management in a changing environment.

Chapter 2: The Concept of Management

In a changing environment, we will consider some of the significant tasks that managers are expected to undertake and also consider some of the barriers that make change difficult to manage. Terms such as 'stakeholder' (and stakeholder analysis) quasi-market, competition and collaboration will be considered through the use of exercises and activities. The management role of facilitating change will be considered as a planning activity that the reader can locate within their own practice area.

Chapter 3: Managing and Leading in Different Environments

As Chapter 1 and 2 will show, social work managers need the skills and abilities to manage within many different contexts. Chapter 3 will consider those different and changing environments. As part of a management team, social work managers will work with colleagues throughout the organisation who may all share the same professional background. However, equally, social work managers will manage teams made up of personnel from different disciplines or sit on management boards that include different professional groups. From a team perspective, some staff will be permanent members of the organisation whilst others may be temporary or transient workers. It has to be acknowledged that the 'mix' of teams today is often complex and unstable and this means that the management role is also complex with different demands and different levels of motivation. The social work manager, however, has the task of ensuring that teams function and do what they are set up to do within the chaos of a volatile and sometimes 'messy' environment. The use of activities and exercises will help the reader make sense of this complexity and consider differing roles, responsibilities and cultures.

Chapter 4: The Influence of Policy

Over-regulation and the burden of policy and procedures are often considered as obstacles to professional practice. We will consider these concepts and their influence on practice and their importance. We discuss how policies and procedures are both drivers and implementers of change. From a management perspective, this chapter will give the social work manager some thoughts as to how policies are implemented, delivered and evolve. In the following chapter we will look at how the concept of identity is enacted within an environment of change and uncertainty.

Chapter 5: Identity and Culture

We begin by defining 'identity' with a general explanation that will then be refined within a professional sphere. We will consider some of the theories used to explain professional identity and look at how we can maintain professional identity through external and internal change including how professional identity is enacted within the organisation but also in our dealings with service users and other stakeholders. We will examine the gaps in social work practice between what we want to do, what we are expected to do and what we can do. The social work manager is asked by their team to fill the gaps or explain them in a way which allows the worker to maintain identity and 'reason to practice' whilst also maintaining their own. Resulting tensions will be explored within a context of change.

Chapter 6: Managing Performance

For the social work manager it seems that there are many expectations. How does the social work manager manage the performance of the individual team member, the team that can be diverse and changing, the organisational demands as well as the demands of the external environment of service users and other stakeholders? This chapter will unravel what is meant by 'performance management' and look at strategies that can combine these demands with the management function and good practice outcomes. The use of activities and exercises will aid the reader towards a clear understanding of the complexity of managing performance.

Chapter 7: Personal and Professional Development

So far we have considered how the social work practitioner and manager can manage within a changing environment using knowledge, tools, techniques and strategies. However, social care organisations are made up of people with unique and differing needs. We may have the tools to be effective but, equally, staff members need to feel that their needs are listened to, acknowledged and satisfied in order that they can understand the realities of their working environment and role. We will consider the complexity of motivation in its broadest sense and how this impacts on individuals, teams and organisations. We will discuss, with the use of activities and exercises, how managers can motivate their staff members within the changing structure and culture of social work and social care by the effective use of supervision, networking and knowledge sharing.

Chapter 8: The Influence of Self: Towards a New Reality?

In our conclusion we consider a vision for the future. We contend that, regardless of where a social worker or social care worker is within the hierarchy of the organisation, the reality is that all practitioners are managers: managers of their own work practices, managers of their own cases, managers of their teams and managers of social care organisations. This chapter will propose a new social work identity and structure of work that is much broader and encompassing than previously recognised or acknowledged. We have talked about change and managing change throughout this book and it is that change which necessitates a more advanced and perhaps more sophisticated social work identity – one which crosses the boundaries of practice and management. As part of this new identity, social workers need to embrace aspects of professional confidence, professional development, professional vision, professional values and ultimately professional communities. This chapter recognises the influence of policy as a driver of the future of social work and management, but goes one step further by offering a more empowering opportunity for social work practice, in which the knowledge and skills of practitioners and managers can positively contribute to the changing nature and setting of service delivery.

CHAPTER 1

The Challenges of Change

Key themes in this chapter include:
Change
Change and social work practice
Modernisation
Drivers of change
Understanding change
Reactions to change

Introduction: Change, and what we need to know

We live and work in a world that appears to be in constant change. Everyday something changes, sometimes for the better, sometimes for the worse. It is often hard to keep up with the changes that are happening around us.

Some people see change as continuous development and improvement, whilst for others it is a frightening step into the unknown. Perhaps your first venture into social work felt a bit like that. Yet life, after all, is about change. We cannot be forever walking on the spot; that is called 'marking time'. As Martin and Henderson (2001) point out, health and social care is no longer concerned with maintaining the status quo but rather about stimulating and encouraging change and innovation in order to make continuous improvement. This is a positive way of looking at change. Change, from this perspective, can no longer be conceived of as a one-off event or temporary adjustment, but must be seen as a continuous process of adaptation to flux in the environment (Hartley et al., 1997). Whatever your role or work location, being able to cope with change is likely to be a requirement of all social workers and is, therefore, important to understand and highly relevant to your professional role.

Activity 1.1
Reflect on a change that you have experienced in your life and think about the following:

- Was the change a one-off event or part of a continuous process?
- How did you manage that change?
- Did you feel you had any control over the change that was happening?
- What helped you adapt to differences as a result of the change?

The General Social Care Council statements (2002) describe codes of practice and standards of professional conduct together with a set of professional beliefs. These implicitly encapsulate the values and ethical base that underline what is important and what is right when practising social work. Clearly, an evolving organisation will affect the nature of the social work task but should not detract from the underlying social work principles. Change within a social care setting may be interpreted as 'modernisation' and that, in itself, may be a positive change. However, modernisation should not be achieved at the expense of devaluing social work standards of practice. It is not a failure on the part of professionals to embrace the principle of 'modernisation' that is at issue, but rather, to balance the need for change against a need to conserve core values. So, where there is a gap between professional values and organisational requirements there is a greater risk, therefore, of professional alienation. Is this professional paranoia or are there grounds for professional concern?

Figure 1.1

Consider the above scales that are showing an even balance between change and social work values. One is not rising above or pushing down the other. Perhaps this is the ideal?

Activity 1.2
From your own practice experience where do you feel the scales are set?
- Who or what determines the drivers of where the scales are set?
- Is there a significant gap between modernisation and change and social work core values?
- Do you feel professionally alienated as a result?
- What needs to happen to return to a state of equilibrium?

Social work as a profession has an uneasy relationship with politicians and distrust on both sides seems likely. Johnson, quoted in Powell (1999: 97) believes that Labour's policies on personal social services reflect antipathy and a mistrust of professionalism in general. More succinctly, the problem with social work is perhaps that its existence is a permanent reminder to politicians of their failure to deal with social and political issues. One might argue that the fear of social work as a profession has allowed itself to become an instrument of ministerial will. The role of social work as 'agent of change' can be a very uncomfortable one, delivering initiatives in a political environment that distrusts its competency and effectiveness, to a community of service users that distrusts its power and authority. Social workers have had to learn to manage this tension within their own practice but doing so can sometimes be a draining and demoralising experience. Sadly, for some, tension and contradiction pass a point of no return and qualified, experienced and 'good' social workers leave the profession because they feel professionally alienated.

Towards integration

Does integration mean change?

> Activity 1.3
> Experience suggests that many people who use social services also rely on other public services, for example, health, housing, employment services and benefit agencies. The problems people experience are often connected and it is important to ensure that the services they receive are well co-ordinated. Consider a service user with whom you may currently be working with. Placing the service user in the centre, map out all the professional networks that may be involved.

In the 1980s and 1990s, policy was dominated by attempts to separate the purchasing and provision of services and to apply the principles of market capitalism to the welfare state (Loney et al., 1991). Since the election of the Labour government in 1997, policy has shifted to one which is increasingly dominated by the integration of health and social care by breaking down organisational and professional barriers to create change that promotes a more 'efficient', 'user-friendly' and 'safe' service. Terms such as 'joined up services', 'a multi-professional approach', 'inter-professional collaboration' have become part of government rhetoric but what do these terms really mean and do they always promote positive change?

Through policies that promote integration, the government is trying to achieve two key changes:

- First, it wants to give greater responsibility for planning and delivery of services to 'local' areas through general practitioners, primary care and hospital trusts. In doing so, the government believes that partnership and participation between providers and users of services can be improved;
- Second, it aims to eliminate differences between areas in terms of standards of services. As a direct result we see the growth of inspection and standard setting regimes.

The belief is that health and social care can be more effective working together rather than independently. Being 'joined up' means recognising the wholeness of people's lives (Social Services Inspectorate, 2000) and few would disagree with this, although it is not a new idea and underpinned the reforms of the early 1970s that led to the creation of Social Services Departments in England and Wales. It is not, however, historical and cultural differences alone that present obstacles to achievement of synergy between health and social care and other agencies but rather failure to address the totality of change that goes beyond setting mutually determined strategic objectives. Significantly, the financial pressures in health and social care lead to an innate tendency to defend territories and budgets. Availability of resources, different methods or approaches of organisational and financial systems, different accountabilities and constraints stemming from different perceptions of status and priorities at practitioner level, remain to be addressed. One example is the current debate about the differences between providing health and social care for elderly people. Arguably, most of the distinctions are spurious and largely management creations that support different ways of controlling budgets through rationing services. The hope that these differences will simply resolve themselves in time is at best optimistic and at worst complacent.

None of this is an argument against integration of services but it is also to recognise that much has yet to be tackled. Research suggests that better outcomes for service users with even the most complex needs are achieved through integrated assessments and care plans. These will need to be developed upon evidence-based protocols specifying the roles, responsibilities and sequencing of interventions by the different professionals involved. This requires integrating processes, such as single assessment frameworks, that result in the organisation and delivery of services that are truly multi-agency, financed through joint budgets and management structures. It is important that health and social-care services cease to be dominated by fragmented responses and communication that is too frequently superficial and disconnected.

Activity 1.4
Consider the case of Mrs Green, who is an 84-year-old lady, and normally lives at home alone with the support of carers. Mrs Green sustained a fall at home which resulted in an emergency admission to hospital. As the case managing social worker you have undertaken an assessment and consider that the care that Mrs Green should receive at home needs to be increased in order to ensure her safety and prevent further falls. You feel that Mrs Green should not return home until the extra provision is in place. This necessitates an increase in funding which takes time to secure. The health authority, however, are putting pressure on you as they 'need the bed'.

Referring back to the balance between modernisation, change and social work values, consider also the dimension of working with other agencies who also have competing demands.

How might you respond to the needs of other agencies, given your own need, to secure the best possible outcome for service users?

Drivers of change

First, what do we mean by 'drivers of change'? One approach is to think of these under three headings; political, social and economic.

Political

A key point to remember in identifying political drivers of change is that the introduction of new legislation and government initiatives will always have an influence on organisational structures, professional practice and services to users and carers.

Care services in the United Kingdom, for example, have undergone significant changes following the integration of health and social care, as part of the government's reform of the National Health Service (Health Act, 1999; NHS Plan, 2000). These changes have led increasingly to social workers working as members of multi-disciplinary teams and the development of joint practices such as the single assessment process, outlined in the *National Service Framework for Older People* (DoH, 1999). We will return to this in Chapter 3.

The White Paper, *Our Health, Our Care, Our Say: A New Direction for Community Services* (2006) sets a new direction for community services aimed at turning the vision of the Green Paper *Independence, Well-being and Choice: our vision for the future of social care for adults in England* (2005) into reality. The new vision for health and social care promotes more personalised care that aims to provide an opportunity for people to assess their own needs, supported by direct payment initiatives. It remains to be seen how the vision for developing adult services is able to compete with other government funding pressures, but each of these initiatives in practice build upon principles of joint working, commissioning and organisational structures.

In children's services, proposed changes to the organisation of provision culminated in the Children Act 2004 (DfES, 2004) along with a number of publications under the heading *Every Child Matters* (2003). Children's Trusts bring together social care, education and health into a single structure to ensure services are child centred and such integration will, when fully implemented, have an important influence on how agencies work together.

In the field of learning disabilities, *Valuing People* (DoH, 2001) has been instrumental in promoting greater service-user consultation and partnership while the introduction of *Fair Access to Care Services-guidance on eligibility criteria for adult social care* (2003) sets out approaches aimed at achieving greater consistency in determining eligibility criteria, assessment and charging for services.

After the implementation of the Community Care (Direct Payments) Act 1997 local authorities were given the power to make direct cash payments to meet the assessed needs of disabled people. These payments were to be in lieu of community care services formerly provided under the National Health Services and Community Care Act 1990. Legislation was extended to older people in 2000 and again in 2001 to carers of disabled children.

Each of these Acts, and there are many others, are examples of political drivers of change that influence the setting and practice of social work. They provide new opportunities and challenges but also give rise to uncertainties and risks that are a feature of all change.

Finally, changes in power at local or central government level will inevitably lead to different approaches and policy initiatives to address the social care agenda. The nature of politics, however, has changed fundamentally over the past decade and traditional values that separated the major political parties are less easily defined. The debate is now more centred around issues rather than ideological differences and the old style differentiation between 'left' and 'right' or control and liberty.

> ### Activity 1.5
> Through an in-depth analysis of one of the policies identified above, answer the following questions:
>
> 1. What was or who were the drivers behind the creation of the policy?
> 2. What are the significant changes identified?
> 3. Who are the main stakeholders who have a vested interest in the successful implementation of this policy?
> 4. What core values can you identify as either explicit or implicit within the policy?
> 5. Can this policy promote positive change?
> 6. What barriers might need to be overcome to ensure positive outcomes?

Social

We turn now to social drivers of change. Increasing life expectancy will lead to greater demands on health and social care services. Within the next decade 25 per cent of the UK population will be aged over 65 years, with a resultant 20/30 per cent increase in dependency (Scase, 2000). Within this group the proportion of people aged 85 years or above has increased from 7 per cent in 1971 to 12 per cent in 2004 (Social Trends, 2005).

It is self-evident that an ageing population in the UK influences service demands – particularly services such as home care that assist people to remain living in their own home and to function as independently as possible. An estimated 415,000 service users received home support in 2000 and the number of contact hours purchased or provided by the local authority home support service increased by 77 per cent (Social Trends, 2005). There has also been a major shift in provider patterns. As with residential home places the independent sector provides much of the care, around 64 per cent in 2002, with funding provided by the local authority. The social model of care aimed at promoting independence and choice seems overly optimistic, against a backcloth of increased demand, higher dependency levels, financial constraints and profound structural and organisational change. Evidence from surveys in 2002/2003 revealed that two thirds of 60-74 year old men and three fifths of women of the same age, who reported that they had difficulties with daily activities or mobility, received no help from any source, paid or unpaid (Social Trends, 2005).

In the past, a significant share of responsibility for caring for disabled and elderly people was undertaken within the family. The growth of single households, the increasing proportion of women engaged in full-time as well as part-time jobs, and the growing complexity of personal relationships through separation and divorce will, according to Scase (2000), make care within the family even less an option in the future.

In addition to demographic forces, other changes in the external environment such as advancements in technology, changing working practices, homelessness (which has more than doubled between 1997 and 2004) are likely to create additional demands on state resources and care services. It is little wonder that the government is keen to emphasise greater self-responsibility in planning for the future.

Activity 1.6
Look up a demographic table from the web site http://www. statistics.gov.uk/socialtrends)

By considering the most significant tables you have found relating to Social Trends, draw up a list of social changes most likely to influence the profession of social care and the role of the social worker.

How might the service have to change to meet the changes you have identified?

Economic
From the analysis of social trends we can see how the likely shortfall between available resources and demand will act as an economic driver for future policy change. Indeed, the cynic might suggest that the government policy of

integration in health and social care is, to a large extent, influenced by the potential for 'economies of scale' savings. Similarly, the introduction of the single assessment process for older people, as part of the National Service Framework for Older People (DoH, 2001) can be seen to have both a service and a cost benefit objective. Such misrepresentations of policy initiatives stem from deeply held concerns about funding shortfalls and it may be no coincidence that community care was once thought to be the 'cheaper option' which it has certainly not turned out to be.

Rummery (2002) rightly makes the point that the social worker's legal obligation to their employer imposes a responsibility on them to ration services through screening, eligibility criteria and targeting greatest need. While these are standard management techniques aimed at controlling the imbalance between supply and demand, they present professional dilemmas for social workers charged with being 'needs led' in a financial climate that invariably falls short of meeting these aspirations. For many years, social care services have been stuck in this vicious circle of having to invest in responding to 'the greatest need' within the context of child protection, looked after children and residential provision across the service specialisms. This has been at the expense of longer-term preventative services and thus drivers of change have too frequently, it can be argued, been concerned with actions aimed at managing financial pressures.

Cost control is an essential function of any business and, in the absence of new approaches to local government financing, the tension between imposing mechanisms to manage demand and meeting assessed need will remain. Indeed, for the social worker it may feel that social objectives are usually secondary to financial and economic ones, or are not strictly objectives at all, but rather a means of controlling expenditure. Rhetoric about empowerment and choice may simply mask the politically expedient need to avoid confronting the difficult issue of raising taxes. Whether people are prepared to pay higher taxes, make provision through personal insurance or enhanced means tested charges for services, remains to be seen. In the meantime, this is a significant driver of change that mirrors the wider conflict between the organisational need to control expenditure and the traditional service ethic of social work. As a social work student was heard to observe, 'How long will it be before only the deserving are entitled to a service and who will define who is or who is not deserving?'

Influence of the modernisation agenda

How does change affect performance?

One big trouble which social services have suffered from is that up to now no government has spelled out exactly what people can expect or what staff are expected to do. Nor have any clear standards of performance been laid down. This government is to change all that. We propose to set new standards of performance.

(DoH, 1998)

The White Paper, *Modernising Social Services* (DoH, 1998) required all local authority social services departments to undertake a massive overhaul of the way services were delivered. At the same time, an avalanche of key policy directives and expectations about 'modernising' appeared, some of which we illustrated in identifying political initiatives that have been instrumental in driving change. Indeed, the modernisation agenda can be said to have strengthened the resolve of social work to be regarded as a profession.

The 'third way' is employed by the present government to capture a distinctive approach to driving up efficiency and effectiveness in the personal social services. *Modernising Social Services* (DoH, 1998) defines the 'third way' as lying between the commercialisation of care provision that characterised the Conservative government reforms, and the near monopoly held by local authorities in the field of social care during the 1960s and 1970s.

Activity 1.7

The 'third way' was seen to be underpinned by a number of important principles:

- That care provided should support independence and respect dignity.
- Services should meet individual need and people have a say in what services they get and how they are delivered.
- That services should be accessed, organised, provided and financed in a fair, open and consistent way.
- Children looked after by the local authorities should get a decent start in life.
- Social care staff will be sufficiently trained and skilled.
- Social services should work to clear acceptable standards.

(DoH, 1998: para. 18)

Based on your current practice experience, how many of the above principles have been achieved? Can you identify any barriers to these seemingly positive statements of change?

Cree (2002: 23) summarises the 'third way' as, 'one that would promote independence, improve consistency, ensure quality of opportunity to children (especially in relation to education), protect adults and children from abuse or neglect in the care system, improve standards in the workforce and improve delivery and efficiency'.

These underpinning principles of policy are ones to which social workers can subscribe and while there will always be debate around the notion of 'commercialisation', it is not ideological indifference that most influences implementation of these objectives but failure to invest in infrastructures essential to expansion and diversification in any business. As a consequence, there remain serious doubts that, despite the rhetoric of optimism, sufficient knowledge and skills exist in the independent market place. Furthermore, there are insufficient public sector resources available to encourage and facilitate the development of viable commercial suppliers. The risk for local authorities is that loss of market control, through over reliance on a limited number of independent providers, will ultimately lead to higher unit costs for care.

It would be wrong, however, to lay the blame on local authorities alone. One could argue that perhaps a measure of New Labour's ambivalence towards social services is that it has not provided sufficient resources to meet the changing expectations arising from the policy drivers of 'modernisation'. Indeed, the government's pre-occupation with evaluation and monitoring performance has served to re-enforce the tendency for local authority social services to become more engaged in assessing risk and resources, contracting services and enforcing compliance (Horner, 2003). In this respect they are in line with the Conservative reform agenda that shifted the emphasis of public sector social services away from provision of care towards planning, purchasing, prioritising and rationing.

Empowerment and choice are at the heart of public sector reform yet for service users and carers, these have to a large extent been sacrificed to rationing of scarce resources, assessment of means and risk, managerialism and financial pressures. It is difficult to achieve choice in financially pressurised local authorities who come to rely on pre-selected packages of care that are not really tailored to individual need.

Understanding change

Despite the potential positive outcomes, change is often resisted. As long ago as 1970, Toffler referred to the 'future shock' of change, suggesting that people are naturally wary of change. Care service providers, like all organisations, face new challenges over time and we have identified a number of these arising from political, social and economic drivers. Future chapters will elaborate on these further.

In discussing organisational change we can talk about either small (micro) change or large (macro) change. For example, we can talk about how a small team goes about implementing a new way of communicating with each other in order to promote best practice through information sharing within their team, or, on the other hand, we can talk about major change within an organisation where there is a need to change all or parts of the whole infrastructure, including systems, procedures and culture. Within private sector organisations this may involve strategies to increase productivity or output when decisions for change are based on economics and the wish to realise profit. As we have seen, drivers of public sector change are concerned with social profit, that is to say, change initiatives to improve the quality of services to the public, and to strengthen their role in developing partnership arrangements. The difficulty for local authorities has been in managing the need to simultaneously combine and balance social objectives, structural change and increased demand against a backcloth of under-funding.

A complex, diverse and rapidly changing environment has led to local authority organisations facing transformational rather than incremental change. Transformational change, as Rumelt states (1995: 115) is: 'The process of engendering a fundamental change in an organisation with the goal of achieving a dramatic improvement on performance'.

Incremental change refers to a strategy of change which is planned over time, in stages, like steps rising upwards where an initial small change occurs followed by a plateau before another step change.

Language also changes as new influences are brought to bear on service providers. The words we use become part of current fashion, as in, for example, 'seamless service', 'working in partnership', 'joined up services' and 'modernisation'. Jargon can sometimes make it feel as if changes are happening when in reality they are not. After all, there is nothing new about working in partnership with others. So what is the nature of this change? To begin with, the influence of managerialism, integration of services, commissioner and provider arrangements that have replaced directly managed services, expansion of independent provision and a major shift from institutional care towards community based approaches, have all significantly contributed to new structures and practices in health, social services and voluntary organisations. These ideas will be developed further in Chapter 5 when we discuss identity and culture.

Other macro and micro influences

The changes identified above are by no means the only factors to impact on social work practice. Introduction of performance management, greater responsibility and accountability and increased administrative and procedural requirements have also contributed. Indeed, it could be argued that policies and procedures with too many prescribed outcomes have led to dictating to practitioners not only how they should work but the rationale they should follow (Jordan, 1990). What social workers are able to do depends on where the referral stands in terms of eligibility priority, statutory or legal obligations, the availability of staff and physical resources. There is no room for unquestioned assumptions and 'common sense' notions that some practitioners have come to rely on. Central to these changes is a requirement that social workers 'move away from the vague, invalidated and haphazardly derived knowledge traditionally used in social work toward a more systematic, rational and empirically-oriented development and use of knowledge for practice' (Fisher, 1993: 14). This is demonstrated through the emergence of evidence based approaches and reflective practice that provides a link between the high ground of theory and 'swampy lowlands' of practice (Schon, 1983). Reflection in this context is an intellectual activity in which the practitioner is able to look back on past experiences of practice to bring personal understanding to their experience that can be used to inform future practice. It is no less an activity for social workers as a means of exploring their own reactions to change.

Partnership and change

Another way to understand the practice implications of change is through the way we respond to problems and difficulties. These can be viewed in terms of the movement that has occurred from:

- Doing things to service users.
- Doing things for service users.
- Doing things with service users.

Throughout the assessment process, the professionals involved, and the family, should be working together with a view to establishing joint agreement on the nature of the problem and what actions are necessary to meet the needs identified. Working together in this way provides for greater consistency, more informed outcomes and less duplication of activities between agencies.

The principle of working in partnership is now well established but the term is meaningless without clarity about its purpose, limits, boundaries and the outcomes it is hoped to achieve. Communication is the foundation to all partnerships and the social worker who fails to provide service users with information, engage in shared decision making and acknowledge the extent of their powers (which includes what they cannot do as well as what they can) is unlikely to be working in partnership. It is important to remember that few of us communicate as well as we think we do.

Partnership is not just about working with service users but includes collaboration with other professionals and agencies. Indeed, what is distinctive about New Labour's position on partnership is that it is a central idea in managing public services (Ling, 2000). *Working Together to Safeguard Children* (DoH, 2006) and the *Framework for the Assessment of Children in Need and their Families* (DoH, 2000) set out ways in which local authorities and other agencies need to work together to protect children. In adult services, the Health Act (1999) identified ways in which health and social care organisations could work in partnership, for example, through lead commissioning whereby one authority takes on responsibility for purchasing a service on behalf of other organisations. Other examples include shared budgets between health and social care and moves toward structural integration which extends the partnership principle to one of permanency. All these initiatives, and there are many others, demonstrate central government's commitment to 'working together'.

In spite of government expectations and numerous policy and procedural guidelines, collaboration and partnership across organisational and professional boundaries remain inherently difficult (Henderson and Atkinson, 2003). Partnership can be used to justify many approaches and working together is easy when things are going well. Where there are underlying conflicts of interest, tensions arise because different people want different things out of a situation. For example, where there are different responsibilities and different budgets the need for each organisation to manage and protect finite resources can become an overriding consideration. The degree of priority given by a hospital doctor to free up an urgently needed bed will be different from that of a social worker aiming to first ensure that appropriate community care arrangements are set in place.

Essentially, partnership working is about improving outcomes for service users. It would be a mistake, however, to regard organisational differences as manageable through top-down structural approaches. It may also be unwise to believe that support for the principle of partnership is sufficient to achieve necessary changes in professional relationships and practices. We can illustrate these differences through comparisons between health and social care.

Social care sits alongside a range of services provided by local authorities but subject to local decision making. The National Health Service is a nationally organised service. Health remains by and large free at the point of delivery while many services provided by local authorities are means tested. Social care is increasingly dominated by commissioning arrangements and the mixed economy but health remains a largely in-house provision. Social work is dominated by a single profession whereas the National Health Service is made up of various professions each with a degree of autonomy which is sometimes experienced by social care colleagues as authoritarian and disempowering.

Activity 1.8

Consider the below quotation:

It's not about losing power to another agency, its about losing your job or not being able to do what makes the job worthwhile -losing your credibility and losing the ability to be human still.

(Dimmock, 2002: 10)

What do you think this statement means?
- Does change in how and where services are provided equate to 'losing credibility' and 'ability to be human'? (Perhaps the simplest response to this question is 'it depends' on the nature of change, individual reactions and, importantly, how it is managed.)

- Reflect on a practice situation where you have worked within a multi-professional capacity. How were professional skills and knowledge respected but also shared for the best outcome for the service user?

It is clear from our study thus far that differences can occur at four levels: organisational, policy, practice and service delivery, and each can present challenges to working relationships. Structural approaches seem likely to be less successful in the immediate term than working relationships developed at grass-roots level, built on understanding and trust. Knowing what works and why, and addressing first what gets in the way, is no straightforward task, but one essential to developing partnership arrangements that are able to demonstrate real difference through improved service outcomes.

Social workers have an opportunity to shape and deliver services in roles that require the synergy of both managerial and professional skills, contributing to an agenda of integration at different levels in public, private and voluntary organisations. We have yet some way to go and the foreseeable future is likely to be one characterised by continuous change and resultant uncertainty for social workers.

Management style and its influence on change

One of the most important factors in the successful management of change is the style of professional management behaviour. Some service users, as with some staff, may actually prefer, and respond better, to others taking control. In most cases, however, the introduction of change is more likely to be effective with a participative style of managerial behaviour. Similarly, social work practice acknowledges the value of working alongside service users in planning and implementing personal change. An important priority is to create an environment of trust, ownership and shared commitment.

Doyle et al. (2000) undertook a study of 92 managers from 14 public sector organisations and from 14 private organisations. The research addressed six themes:

- communication
- evaluation
- learning
- attitudes
- relationships
- change implementation

The research findings suggested that managing change in the public sector had been experienced as more pressured than in the private sector.

Among the negative elements of the change process identified by Doyle were:

- Inadequate employee involvement and poor management-employee relationship.

- Little innovation in employee communication.
- Lack of systematic pre-planning, monitoring and assessment of change.
- Likely consequences from change not explored and anticipated.
- Employee views are not considered when assessing change.
- Those affected by change are not given adequate time to adjust.
- There is not enough time to reflect on the lessons of change.
- Repeat mistakes in change implementation are common.
- Middle and senior managers work with different assumptions about change.

All of these can and do create barriers to change, which need to be overcome, if change is to be successful and effective.

> **Activity 1.9**
> Reflect on a situation in your working life where a manager has had to manage change. Perhaps you were that manager. Consider the above statements in turn and reach a conclusion as to whether managing change was effective in this case.

Reactions to change

When a change is announced, the first response is often one of indifference. The announcement does not seem to sink in. Nothing happens. Social workers continue to work as usual in the belief that 'it probably won't affect what I do' or 'I'll worry about it when it happens'. As we identified earlier in this chapter, changes in organisational policy influence practice and therefore will always impact on what social workers do. This initial reaction is characteristic of the denial stage and is harmful because it gets in the way of understanding the reasons for change and responding to the implications, both personally and professionally. Resistance to change is not intrinsically bad if it leads to the review of ill-advised plans (Thompson, 2003).

Resistance to change can take many forms and it is sometimes difficult to identify the exact reasons, although these may include:

- Fear of the unknown. Changes in the work situation present a degree of uncertainty and apprehension as in 'Will I be able to cope'? 'Is my job at risk'? 'I may lose job satisfaction'.
- Financial implications. 'Will it require additional work for the same level of pay'? Fear that change may lead to the reduction, directly or indirectly, to pay or other benefits.
- Loss of freedom. If change is seen as likely to prove inconvenient or result in increased control.
- A desire not to lose something of value and the belief that change will not enhance services to users and carers.

From the initial stage of denial, people begin to experience a number of emotions: self-doubt, anger, anxiety, and frustration being the most common.

These can be accompanied by a lot of grumbling and threats to seek jobs elsewhere. Colleagues become pre-occupied with the thought of change, and it is interesting to reflect on how much easier it is to manage change when it is not your change. These may seem rather negative reactions, since there are those who relish change and see it as a challenge and respond with positive enthusiasm. Nevertheless, for others there will be the wish to retain old and comfortable ways because they are familiar and give a feeling of security.

Calculating how change might be received within an organisation makes an important contribution to informing implementation. Lewin (1951) introduced the notion of Force Field Analysis which identified driving forces for change and restraining forces that work against change.

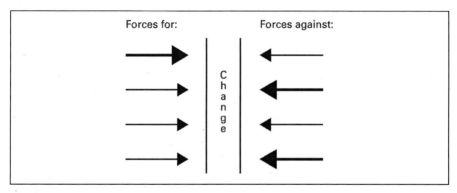

Figure 1.2   Force Field Analysis

While this can be seen as a helpful management tool to calculate the advisability of different approaches to change and their likely level of support, it is also a method that social workers can employ to view change from a service delivery perspective and thus contribute to a more informed response to change proposals.

Activity 1.10
Lewin (1951) developed a three phase process of behaviour modification necessary to managing a programme of planned change:

1. **Unfreezing** – reducing those forces that maintain behaviour in its present form. This involves recognition of the need to change.
2. **Movement** – development of new attitudes or behaviour and implementation of change.
3. **Refreezing** – stabilising change at the new level and reinforcement through supporting mechanisms, for example, supervision.

In what circumstances have you encouraged others to 'unfreeze' or 'unlearn' something or some behaviour, before you have been able to help them accept change? How easy was this process?

Helping individuals or groups face up to change involves taking them through the crisis stage towards real acceptance of the need to change. By now, you will have identified the similarities between organisational change and changes that impact on the lives and experiences of service users. The circumstances may be different but the emotions and feelings are likely to be much the same.

Figure 1.3 below shows various stages experienced during a typical change.

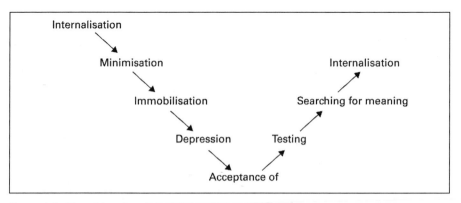

Figure 1.3 Transitional model of change

Internalisation: Standardised accepted behaviour until change announced.

Minimisation: To deny the importance of change. Denial is a normal human reaction to change. Temporary retreat.

Immobilisation: Sense of being overwhelmed – frozen – unable to act and unable to understand.

Depression: As staff face the implications of change – having to forge new skills and relationships.

Acceptance: At this stage staff begin to let go of the old state of being, with the acceptance that there is no going back.

Testing: New behaviour to cope with new situations – self image.

Searching for meaning: Reflective stage (rather than acting) i.e. why things are different.

Internalisation; Meanings discovered – becomes part of ordinary behaviour.

Eventually, everyone reaches a low point and begins to move up the other side of the change curve: an indication that things are getting better (Hopson and Adams, 1976).

Activity 1.11
Some suggestions for personal management of change:
- First, fully understand what is being proposed.
- Re-frame from personal to service user perspective.
- Identify the personal and professional challenge, seeking solutions.
- Contributing from the inside is better than shouting from outside. Be a part of the discussion.
- Use as a 'learning approach' – explore differences as they can be opportunities for learning and professional debate.
- Predicting a stressful event usually reduces its severity and understanding reduces fear and apprehension.
- Value team members.
- Be prepared to challenge change but be prepared also to change yourself.

From your experience, identify the factors that have been significant in the following changes in your team or organisation:
- A successful change.
- An unsuccessful change.
- An externally imposed change.

Summary

This chapter has sought to identify and demystify the concept of change by touching on some of the current discussions, debates and theories. We have seen that change is all around us all of the time. Sometimes change is so subtle that we hardly notice it happening whilst at other times change can be significant, explicit and transformational. We have noted that the effects of change are similarly experienced in both a public, professional context as they are in a personal situation. Invariably, if people do not think that change will significantly affect them, then they generally dismiss it. As such, change can be seen as a concept of action with consequence and effect.

As social workers, we are influenced by the external world in which we operate. The external world outside of the workplace is influenced by such things as economics, politics, social change and trends. This external world permeates the boundaries of our workplace, through the legislation, policies and practices that we use, and the 'way we do things' through the culture of organisations and practice. This, in turn, affects how we work with service users, carers and other vulnerable people in society, and what we are realistically able to do as they too acknowledge and work with either voluntary or imposed change.

We have argued that what we are realistically able to do may not be in line with why we first entered the social work profession. The gap between change through political modernisation strategies and our own professional values may, at times, be wide and difficult to understand and, at such times, we may experience a sense of professional alienation and loss of identity.

The following chapters will expand on some of the most significant issues raised within this introduction and look at how the gap between modernisation and professional values can be bridged.

CHAPTER 2

The Concept of Management

Key themes in this chapter include:
Social workers as managers
The influence of managerialism
New public sector management
Quasi-markets and choice
Characteristics of leadership

Introduction

'Management' carries a number of meanings and, as a result, the expectations of what a manager will do vary. One view is that management is getting things done through others while another view asserts that the job of management is to support the efforts of staff to be fully productive members of the organisation. To most staff, the term 'management' means a group of people who are primarily responsible for making decisions in the organisation. Indeed, Crainer argues (1998: 11) that:

> Management is active, not theoretical. It is about changing behaviour and making things happen. It is about developing people, working with them, reaching objectives and achieving results.

Peter Drucker, who is widely regarded as the guru of management, offers an additional dimension, (1979: 14):

> Management is tasks. Management is discipline but management is about people. Every achievement of management is the achievement of a manager. Every failure is a failure of a manager.

Despite the widespread use of the term and the copious amount written about the subject it is not easy to find agreement on a simple, comprehensive definition of management. However, what we can say is that management relates to all activities of the organisation. It is not a separate, discrete function and neither can it be departmentalised. An organisation cannot have a department of managers in the same way that it can have a department of other specialist services such as older people, child care or disabilities. Management is best seen, therefore, as an activity common to all other functions carried out within the organisation. The overall responsibility is captured by Naylor (1999: 14):

Management is the process of achieving organisational objectives, within a changing environment, by balancing efficiency, effectiveness and equity, obtaining the most from limited resources, and working with and through other people.

Activity 2.1

What are your initial thoughts on what a manager is and what a manager does? From your own perspective of being a manager, or reflecting on other managers that you have worked with, comment on how true you think the above quotation is?

Management and social care

Managing in health and social care is complex and demanding. Although there are many similarities in the work of managers in different types of organisation the health and social care context is very different. One important difference is the value attached to quality human relationships and the principles and values that underpin care practice. Further, social care managers operate in a political environment subject to legislative requirements, statutory controls and procedures that guide the task of caring for vulnerable adults and children. Standards and performance are more difficult to measure than with profitability and very often the managers' role is one of balancing and responding to the potentially conflicting demands of their organisation, service users and carers. This can be particularly difficult when there are not sufficient resources to ensure standards are met. One marked difference however, between private and public sector managers derives from a study by Arroba and Wedgwood-Oppenheim (1994) who found that local government managers were more committed to organisational objectives and to task achievement which is not supplemented by a concern for interpersonal processes. In local government, the drive, enthusiasm and emphasis on task is exaggerated, while attention to idea generation and interpersonal relationships are less marked. This does not fit easily with government policies promoting the integration of services and intent on breaking down institutional and professional barriers.

Much of the practice of management includes techniques, processes and theories intended to inform practice and, although not all easily fit the particular demands of health and social care, there are a number of common activities and concerns that apply to both private and public sector organisations. There are a number of functions that help define all forms of management. We can divide these activities into five functions: planning, organising, controlling, motivating and leadership. Other people in the organisation may carry out these activities either routinely or periodically and the differences may be of degree rather than type of activity.

Activity 2.2
Take each of the five functions identified below and relate each one to a situation which has necessitated change. This may be in a practice, team or organisation setting:
Planning _____
Organising _____
Controlling _____
Motivating _____
Leading _____
Of the five functions listed above what do you consider to be the most important and why?

The assertion that social workers are also managers may not sit easily with practitioners. It is indicative of social workers that they regard management as an activity divorced from the 'real world' of professional practice. Stereotypically, the manager is a person driven by policy initiatives from central government and achievement of organisational objectives aimed at controlling budgetary pressures. One might wonder whether it is the failure of organisations to make the connection between managing and everyday life that has contributed to the development of mystique and cynicism around the activities of higher management in social care.

Watson (1986) views management as both an art and a science but also refers to it as 'magic' in that it engages in expected rituals and 'politics' that involve 'playing the game'. Both may be meaningful in the light of your own experience but essentially management is about people. Helping social workers to understand the rationale behind decisions and, importantly, valuing the contribution practitioners are able to make to the process, are activities managers in social care do less well. This is particularly surprising because, as Couiser and Exworthy (1999) point out, the authority to manage professionals is grounded in the credibility of having been a practitioner. For their part, social workers are having to understand that they are not autonomous practitioners but are subject to local and central government policy objectives and expectations. Managers, on the other hand, who fail to enlist the knowledge and experience of practice to inform the development and implementation of policy, are unlikely to achieve effective outcomes.

The argument for breaking down role demarcations and traditional relationships between management and practice, in favour of creating more integrated roles, is gathering recognition (Couiser and Exworthy, 1999; Gray et al., 1999). Bourne (1979) for example, views management as a set of interrelated activities:

- Forecasting, setting objectives and planning.
- The definition of problems that need to be solved to achieve these objectives.
- Search for various solutions that might be offered to these problems.

- Determination of the best or most acceptable solutions.
- Securing of agreement that such solutions should be implemented.
- Preparation and issue of instructions for carrying out the agreed solutions.
- The execution of solutions.
- An auditing process for checking whether solutions are properly carried out and, if they are, that they really solve the problems for which they were designed.
- The design, introduction and maintenance of the organisational structures which are most appropriate for these activities.

> **Activity 2.3**
> Revisit your thoughts on management that you outlined in Activity 2.1. Now consider the management activities highlighted by Bourne. Were these activities ones that you initially identified? Take the 9 points and rank them in order of importance. Give an explanation of why you ranked them as you did.

Clearly, Bourne's set of activities is of equal relevance to the social work task and can be seen as an extension to the functions that help define all forms of management identified earlier in this chapter. The professional task of assessment, for example, is a series of interrelated actions in which one component leads to the next. Each function can be identified as a separate set of actions but, in practice, the social worker carries out these activities in a complex unified manner within the total process of working with the service user to address specific problems and to understand their causation.

We can relate, then, many practitioner skills to those of the manager. The difference, as Coulshed and Mullander (2006) argue, has been exaggerated by practitioners not knowing what their managers really do and by failures on both sides to appreciate that working to change an organisation is not so far removed from the mainstay of social work itself, for example, striving for change in the life situation of service users.

The influence of managerialism

Targets and performance management are part of an approach to management in the public sector that is sometimes called 'new public sector management' or 'managerialism'. Reference to 'new' is intended to indicate something different from traditional management and in so far as it puts public service values and ethos first, it *is* different. One might ask whether it does so in practice but this is another matter. It is intended, however, to convey more than this since reference to 'new' promotes the notion of 'modernisation' that, as we identified earlier, is central to government public sector policy.

The terms 'managerialism' and 'performance management' are increasingly used to describe features that involve providing services at lower cost through improved efficiency and by techniques borrowed from business. That is, to plan, monitor and evaluate activities in a rigorous way and make comparisons of performance.

The origins of managerialism, however, do not sit with New Labour alone. After all, it was the Conservative government, elected in 1979, who argued that increasing demands on the welfare state was no longer affordable and therefore introduced policies which encouraged development of private provision so as to reduce publicly funded and provided provision. Since New Labour were elected in 1997, the shift from public sector provision has continued alongside policies of partnership, service integration and an emphasis on improved performance measures. All approaches aimed at both improving standards and utilising resources more efficiently. Indeed, New Labour has actively promoted the notion of greater responsibility, for example, by encouraging people to make personal arrangements to supplement state pension provision.

While there are differences in approach adopted by the political parties, with New Labour placing less emphasis on competition, the policy drives of Labour are similar to the Conservative administration. Johnson, cited in Powell (1999) states that New Labour has adopted many of the major principles of conservative policy and the main differences are now in the area of context and tone. However, Clarke and Newman (1997) suggest that competition between the political parties is about which one can best manage the welfare state.

Managerialism – key features

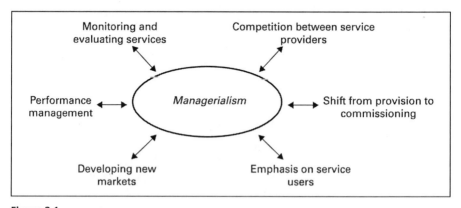

Figure 2.1

Activity 2.4
Consider Figure 2.1. To what extent does your current role include the elements highlighted in Figure 2.1? How do they relate to the

practice setting? How do they relate to the team setting? How do they relate to the organisation setting?

A key characteristic of managerialism is getting the greatest benefit from the resources available. Effective organisations need to have clearly defined objectives and outcomes with targets set to secure them. It follows that there must be performance measures of progress achieved, and performance monitoring to determine success or failure. We will explore this further in Chapter 6.

Quasi-markets and choice

Promoting choice and independence underlies all the Government's proposals.
(DoH, 1989: para. 18)

The concept of choice within public services is very much part of the current political scene. Politicians on both the left and right promote the concept and proposed benefits of enabling consumers of public services to make choices.

The introduction of a quasi-market potentially offers more choice for a service user as services may be purchased by the local authority from a range of service providers drawn from private or independent sectors. Whether it does so in practice is a debatable point.

A quasi-market is both similar to and different from conventional markets. The purchaser, for example, social services, is publicly funded and, unlike a conventional market, the main motivation is not profit but quality of care. In conventional markets consumers spend their own money and can exercise real choice (Henderson and Atkinson, 2003). The introduction of Direct Payments provides this opportunity in social care, although it is still early days and, in many cases, services are purchased on behalf of service users by a care manager or independent organisation operating on behalf of the service user. As Harris (1999) points out, service users are likely to be poor, vulnerable, and unable to 'shop around'.

Activity 2.5

You are the manager of a team that works with elderly service users within the community. You wish to implement a new service of Direct Payments within your team. This is clearly a new initiative and something that the staff group are rather wary about. How can you convince your team that this may be something that is beneficial for service users?

While competition in itself may be a good thing, and in conventional markets as consumers we can expect to reap the benefits both in price and choice, these benefits are not always characteristic of a quasi-market in a social care sector which is struggling to manage the realities of under-funding. Demand is such that services are rationed and, as such, there is a risk that service users receive care that falls short of meeting their physical and emotional needs. Such is the imbalance between supply and demand that financial investment produces only marginal improvements in a rationed service.

Despite the promotion of a 'needs-led' service, resources are set at a level the organisation can afford instead of the level of prevention and enhancement that can promote a good quality of life. There is no discernible difference between the quality of a service and the price paid, and very little capacity or opportunity to move between providers if you are a service user. Furthermore, as Henderson and Atkinson (2003) argue, competition might well increase costs for both purchasers and providers. Where there is a contractual relationship and service specification then contracts must be devised, monitored and enforced. These functions all have professional and administrative implications and represent costly procedures that might, or might not, be off set by savings as a result of competition (Le Grand, 1990).

Quasi-markets are justified on the grounds that they encourage competition which leads to greater efficiency, enhanced consumer choice, diversity of providers and high-quality services. This pre-supposes, of course, that a range of experienced and skilled providers exists in the independent sector, able to meet the local authority's purchasing requirements. While the signs are that the independent sector is responding to the challenge, it is not necessarily a cheaper option, and the search for what some believed was behind a shift from public to independent sector provision. It is also questionable how much choice is available to service users since the number of providers is influenced by the price a local authority is prepared to pay for the service.

Residential and personal support within the community are examples of services which in practice offer users very little choice of provider. Why, for example, would independent providers enter into a contract with a local authority at a unit price below that which they can receive from private demand? In children's services the growth of independent fostering organisations provides high cost services that a local authority has little choice but to purchase, while struggling to maintain an under-funded public sector provision in which foster carers are paid considerably less than their counterparts in the independent sector. Competition in this example has not reduced costs and neither has it significantly improved the ability of an authority to match the needs of children with a range of available placement options.

The fear is that market theory has, in effect, diluted the social worker role to that of purchasing agent, and this is perhaps particularly so in adult services. Drakeford (2000) argues that the social worker has been resurrected as a 'community care manager' of welfare consumption goods which can be traded just like any other commodity in the market place of care. The reality is, however, that no other commodities use 'eligibility criteria assessment' and 'prioritising' to regulate services, and no other brokers of services act in a situation where they have no knowledge about cost. In particular, services for those with special needs, for minorities, or groups which could be perceived as 'difficult', could be seen as financially unattractive for providers to invest in, and therefore consumers and providers may have to pay more to secure services for such groups.

Current shortcomings do not mean we can afford to loose the potential that quasi-markets provide for choice through service diversity and competition. This will not happen, however, without a sustained effort on the part of local authorities to engage in market development, within a framework of collaboration and partnership across professional boundaries, in relation to quantity, quality and cost.

In the meantime social workers in the current climate may well be asking whether a managerialist culture can provide for and sustain the emotional and moral climate in which the skills and sensitivities of care and respect can be practised (Centre for Policy Research, 1998: 13). The danger is that public services might begin to impose traditional market principles and in so doing loose sight of other principles such as fairness, real choice and taking into account the service user's experience.

Activity 2.6
From your experience as a practitioner, a manager and a member of a social care organisation, identify the strengths and shortcomings of a quasi-market from a service user's perspective. From your experience, is a quasi-market always an appropriate response to need?

Planning: the link with practice

One task for both social workers and managers is to bring purpose and meaning to their work. At its very simplest, planning is about setting the direction of something and then guiding activity towards achievement of the plan. In fact, planning is an ordinary every day activity and something all of us do in both our personal and professional lives. For instance, we plan to go on holiday by first thinking about potential destinations: we then consider places of interest; where we might stay; and importantly, whether we can afford it. Once decided we set about making a reservation. This is a simple example of planning but these planning objectives have an additional dimension in professional practice.

There is an important relationship between assessment and planning. Middleton captures this relationship in describing assessment as:

The analytical process by which decisions are made. In a social welfare context, it is a basis for planning what needs to be done to maintain or improve a person's situation . . . Assessment involves gathering and interpreting information in order to understand a person and their circumstances; the desirability and feasibility of change and the services and resources which are necessary to effect it. It involves judgement based on information.

(Middleton, 1997: 5)

All social work activity requires a clear sense of purpose and direction. The plan presents a detailed picture of a situation, those involved and what action might be taken and by whom in order to meet assessed or identified needs and risks. It provides a critical path of activities informed by underpinning concepts which inform good practice. In the past, the objectives of these plans have tended to be defined in terms of service user needs, for example, to continue to receive home care four times a week, or remain in a community home. Pinnock and Garnett (2002) suggest that concentration on services rather than outcomes creates a number of problems:

- Since the plan lacks any clear outcome, it is difficult to establish whether progress has been made.
- Service-led plans tend to encourage dependence on services because they do not recognise the strengths and resources of service users.
- Plans are often self-perpetuating and fail to consider other ways that outcomes might be achieved.

It also has to be said that, while the focus of assessment is 'need', the outcome is increasingly influenced by cost and by resource availability. This can sometimes lead to care being planned in the hope that it will make a difference rather than being able to evidence that it does. By engaging users, carers and other agencies, the social worker is able to develop a statement of purpose with clearly identified and jointly agreed outcomes which include the realities of finite resources.

Effective and competent social workers are constantly challenging their practice and seeking better ways of delivering services while service users and carers will often be the source of ideas for improvement. While some will fall outside the social workers' immediate control, there will be others that can often be implemented at little or no cost. Too often, the importance of the professional relationship can get lost in planning for practical outcomes.

Planning: an organisational perspective

As we have seen, planning has more than one purpose and perhaps the simplest definition is between organisational planning, in which effectiveness can be defined by the degree to which the final outcome of a service or policy match the original objectives, and service planning, aimed at meeting the assessed needs of service users.

The organisation will plan to:

- Provide the best services.
- Meet organisational objectives.
- Make best use of available resources.
- Co-ordinate and manage the budget.

- Prepare for the unexpected.
- Meet changing demands or expectations.

To meet these aims and respond to the drivers of change that we identified in Chapter 1, the organisation needs to plan. It is a myth, however, to believe planning can eliminate change. Changes will happen regardless of what management does but it is a responsibility of management to anticipate changes and to develop the most effective response to them. There are a number of factors, however, that characterise the environment within which local authorities and voluntary organisations operate and which require a planned approach:

- Needs will always exceed supply.
- Services and their costs are never static.
- In a climate of limited resources improved services will depend on better and more productive practices.

Furthermore, corporate planning requires a degree of certainty:

- Local government exists in an uncertain political climate.
- There is uncertainty about resource availability.
- Future demand is difficult to forecast.
- Future level of government grant is unknown.

Inflation imposes more intense pressures on a local authority because a high proportion of expenditure is on employee costs and it is little wonder that many struggle to manage within budgetary limits.

A final thought relates to the way in which services are structured and how these can also contribute to making planning more difficult:

- Social care departments are less integrated than departments in, say, a private company.
- Departments tend to have different goals/objectives because of differences in service user needs and organisational priorities.
- Competition exists for resources.

There are, of course, a number of ways of structuring an organisation to get things done. According to Mintzberg (1981) the most important consideration is not whether it is based on the latest theoretical model, but whether it is the best 'fit' for its aims and objectives. In social care organisations there may be a lack of flexibility or adaptation to changing circumstances and planning for change can seem slow and unimaginative and beset by fixed rules and procedures. However, as we have seen, the influencing factors do not all sit within the gift of the local authority to manage.

It can be hoped that integration policies in social care, education and health will lead to more corporate approaches in service planning. This will depend on the extent to which organisations are able to agree common or overarching goals that form the starting point towards developing a corporate identity, shared values, aspirations and commitment to future direction. What is clear is that integrated planning must be judged in terms of improvements for service users and how well extra demand is accommodated with no increase in the real level of resources. Economies of scale saving will not by itself address this issue. We will explore these ideas in greater depth in further chapters.

Activity 2.7
If you were a senior manager, what actions would you or might you take to ensure that planning was a robust activity within each team or area of service delivery? How would you introduce and implement a new 'effective planning' strategy within your team or organisation without alienating the workforce? What monitoring arrangements would you put in place to ensure that the plans were effective?

Financial planning

As we have seen, local authorities are large, complex organisations, their ability to speedily adjust direction to meet changing demand is a major challenge, and planning can appear ad hoc. We have considered political, social and structural factors that contribute to corporate planning. We will now consider the influence of local authority financing.

Unlike private sector organisations, a surplus or deficit in one year cannot be carried over to the next. What local authorities can spend money on is often determined by ring-fenced monies from central government. That is to say, monies that can only be spent on the purpose for which given. Monies generated from local taxation are relatively modest and there are many competing demands apart from social care. Education, highways and housing, for example.

As we have already established, an additional difficulty for social care is that local authorities are not able to accurately predict expenditure and this adds to the precarious nature of service and budgetary planning. Demand for specialist placements for young people, for example, cannot be foreseen and therefore often represents unplanned expenditure. Moreover, these services are expensive and have a significant impact on the children's services budget.

Another difficulty is that fixed assets appropriate for one client group – buildings, for example, are rarely sufficiently flexible to meet change in demand or service objectives for another service user group. Past failure to invest sufficiently in fixed assets has led many authorities to dispose of their residential care homes to private and independent providers because the capital needs to meet the requisite standards is beyond the local authorities capital budget. The nature of people's needs and thus their involvement with services does not have a tidy beginning, middle and end, but in some cases, contact may extend over a lifetime.

Activity 2.8

As a senior manager within your organisation you have many competing demands for finite financial resources. How do you re-apportion funding? What principles would underpin your decisions?

Influences on voluntary and independent providers

If service planning is difficult for local authorities, it is no less so for voluntary and independent organisations. In the 1970s, voluntary organisations were weak in relation to public services and were dominated by the public sector. The promotion of the mixed economy (National Health Service and Community Care Act, 1990) has produced a range of independent and voluntary sector organisations to support, and in some cases over-shadow, the under-funded and overburdened public services. The growth of independent residential homes and agencies providing personal care for older people, for example, shows a major service shift from public to independent provision.

The informality of past relationships with voluntary organisations has been largely replaced by partnership arrangements which involve the setting of contracts that are sufficiently detailed to include outcomes and quality standards alongside monitoring, compliance and mechanisms to ensure that contracts are fulfilled. Nothing is in itself wrong with that, you might say, since value for money and quality are basic requirements in purchasing goods and services. A more business-like and competitive environment, however, has required a range of managerial skills which have not historically been demanded of voluntary organisations. As a consequence, managers face new challenges (Jackson and Donavan, 1999). Despite the willingness of local authorities to contract out services, few voluntary organisations employ qualified social workers. Indeed, as Coulshed and Mullender (2006) point out, the emphasis on commercial or business 'success' may dictate a different set of priorities and skills for heading up voluntary and independent organisations than those of a qualified social worker. Most significantly the introduction of the contract culture has changed the nature of the voluntary sectors' traditional pioneering, campaigning role to that of mainstream provider. A further difficulty for independent and voluntary sector providers stems from a need, on the one hand, to invest in service infrastructure and, on the other, managing the uncertainties of local authority purchasing requirements.

You may be wondering what this has to do with planning, although the relationship is not as obscure as at first it may appear. A vibrant independent and voluntary sector is essential to the government's objective of a mixed economy, but uncertainties created through the changing nature and level of demand makes it increasingly difficult, as we identified earlier, for a local authority to determine future purchasing and contracting arrangements. In these circumstances investment by independent and voluntary providers in service planning and development becomes an increasingly risky business.

This raises questions about the policy of choice. Choice in this context derives from a market view that says that competition among services leads to improvement, i.e. it will improve provision and reduce price. This will only be so if there are enough services to choose from, and a reluctance on the part of local authorities to become actively engaged in planning service development is therefore to place an over reliance on the voluntary and independent sector to deliver against a backcloth of uncertainty that characterises local authority funding.

Activity 2.9
Using various means, identify and map what services are currently provided in your area by voluntary, non-profit making and charitable organisations. By applying this mapping exercise identify what the service provision gaps are and how you might assist in filling them.

Leadership

The idea of leadership is complex, difficult to capture and open to numerous definitions and interpretations. Handy believes that:

> *Like motivation, the search for the definitive solution to the leadership problem has proved to be another endless quest for the Holy Grail in organisational theory.*

> (Handy, 1993: 97)

Crainer warns that:

> *It is a veritable minefield of misunderstanding and difference through which theoretical practitioners must tread warily.*

> (Crainer, 1995: 8–12)

Yukl argues that:

> *It is neither feasible nor desirable at this point in the development of disciplines to attempt to resolve the controversies over appropriate definitions of leadership . . . definition of leadership is arbitrary and very subjective. Some definitions are more useful than others but there is no 'correct' definition.*

> (Yukl, 1995: 4–5)

One of the many reasons that it is so difficult to agree a definition is because leadership is often tied up with other processes such as power and authority entangled with value judgement (Middlehurst, 1993). Many people believe that leadership is simply being the first, biggest or more powerful, although hierarchical models of leadership based on power are seen to be outmoded with accountability, co-operation and consultation being integral to contemporary models of leadership. Although Yukl (1994) pointed to a lack of consensus about the precise meaning of leadership, he did discern a core agreement across definitions in that it involves a social influence process whereby intentional influence is exerted by one person (or group) over other people.

So are social workers leaders? The idea may at first seem difficult to accept but as we have seen many of the functions of management also describe aspects of the professional task. It could be argued that some form of leadership exists in all groups and if one of the central attributes is social influence then the nature of the social work task implies aspects of leadership. There are other parallels that can be drawn. Mullins (2002: 253) for example, believes leadership is essentially 'a relationship in which one person influences behaviour or actions of others'. In making an application for resources, the social worker exercises leadership in order to influence budget holders. Similarly, the purpose of a child care plan is to influence change where there are concerns about a child's welfare. Leadership is also required to reduce the dissatisfaction which can arise when resource shortfalls lead to service user expectations being unmet. In these circumstances the social worker is required to demonstrate characteristics of leadership through interpersonal behaviour and the process of communication.

Drawing similarities with the professional task in this way may not conform to the traditional hierarchical models of leadership, yet each are activities that contribute to effective functioning, professionally and organisationally. Senge summaries this approach:

> We are coming to believe that leaders are those people who 'walk ahead'; people who are genuinely committed to deep change in themselves and in their organisation. They lead through developing new skills, capabilities, in their understandings. And they come from many places within the organisation.

(Senge, 1996: 45)

Senge's observation draws attention to recent conceptions of leadership as something widely distributed throughout organisations, the central purpose being the empowerment of others. Indeed, it could be argued that leadership is a key facet of the social work task with service users and other agencies. Differences in concepts, Leithwood (2000) concluded, may be accounted for by differences in who exerts influence, its nature and purpose.

There is an important, yet frequently overlooked, relationship between the social work task and that of the manager as 'leader'. It seems less important, however, to debate the similarities and differences than to establish a synergy between practice, vision and service development. In social work and social care it takes practitioners and managers with vision to initiate different ways of meeting assessed need. It also takes vision to shift organisational concern to maintain administrative and procedural conformity. Vision, professionally and organisationally, is about seeing what services could be like while dealing with the realities of today. The fact that leaders have vision and can inspire others is not generally disputed, but, as Westley and Mintzberg state (1989: 21) 'vision comes alive only when it is shared'. Whether the vision of an organisation is developed collaboratively or initiated by others, it becomes the common ground, the shared vision that compels all involved (Murphy, 1988). To regard leadership as exclusively a function of management risks loosing the contribution practice experience is able to make to policy development and service planning.

Characteristics of leadership

The debate about what makes a 'good leader' takes a renewed sense of importance in times of change as organisations search for greater effectiveness and leadership that inspires others and impacts on the organisation in ways that contribute to improved effectiveness. Such aspirations apply no less to the professional task.

Leadership theories generally address the question – Are leaders born or made? Those theorists that accept leaders are born and not made maintain that:

> *There are inborn qualities such as initiative, courage, intelligence and humour which altogether pre-destine a man to be a leader . . . The essential pattern is given at birth.*
>
> (Alder and Rodman, 1991: 14)

Trait theory builds on this view, by concentrating on the personal characteristics of the leader. Traits believed to be characteristic of leaders include all manner of physical, personality and cognitive factors, including height, intelligence and communication skills. Contemporary traits include: self-confidence, empathy, ambition, self-control and curiosity. The most significant of all traits remains 'charisma' although, as Alder and Rodman (1991) point out, not everyone who possesses this will be a leader. In the late 1940s the focus of leadership changed, partly due to disillusionment with the trait theory, and the correlation between certain traits and the capability of leadership was seen to be inconsistent. Another reason for the shift was the emergence of the 'human relations' approach to the study of organisations (Bryman, 1986). During this period, interactionist theories became popular. Social Interactionists held the view that leaders are both born and made, due to the leader requiring certain abilities and skill, but as the situation and the needs of the group changed, so too the person acceptable as a leader changed. An example of this might be the football club manager who is successful with one team but on moving to another team does not enjoy the same level of success.

Doubts surrounding the validity of trait theory gave rise to Fiedler's (1967) notion of contingency and situational approaches. These approaches are grounded in the philosophy that leaders should act as the situation demands. Middlehurst (2000: 21) points out that the importance of Fiedler's ideas lies in their movement away from the notion of individual behaviour being the sole cause of the effectiveness, or failure of leadership. Instead, effectiveness is deemed to depend upon the leader's personality and degree of control over the situation at hand.

The situational approach, therefore, holds that whether a given person becomes leader of a group has less to do with personality, but more to do with such factors as the events and circumstances surrounding the group. In other words, the leader is the person who is in the right place at the right time.

So what do these differences suggest? Clearly, they reflect the complexities referred to at the beginning of this section. Indeed, it seems right to question the notion that there is one type of leader and to argue that leaders vary markedly in personality and behaviour, adopting a variety of approaches in tackling issues. This points to a range of skills and styles that can be deployed to suit particular situations although certain qualities seem central to the task. Adaire (1984) considered that leaders should be good at inspiring others and this depended on their own and others' ability to communicate and share enthusiasm and commitment with others.

Does this take us away from the notion of social workers as leaders? We think not, given that leadership is essentially about relationships with other people, and that you cannot be a leader unless others are prepared to work with you. The social work task too, is about establishing, with others, a shared vision within a relationship that inspires trust and, while responsibilities reflect different levels and roles within an organisation, many practitioner skills in social work are also managerial ones. Perhaps most importantly, the transformational nature of change in health and social care requires, at all levels, a leadership that is able to make sense of complexity in an atmosphere of exceptional ambiguity (Rajan, 2000).

Leadership is therefore about:

- Taking people where they've never been before.
- Inspiring ordinary people to produce extraordinary results.
- Creating a vision of the future that inspires enthusiasm and commitment.
- Setting the strategy to achieve shared objectives.
- Responding to the deep emotions of people as they cope with the journey.
- Encouraging learning by experimentation and tolerating mistakes.

Activity 2.10

Taking each of the above points in turn, answer the following:
- How do these relate to your own thoughts on what leadership is?
- What qualities above do you currently possess?
- What qualities do you feel you need to develop?
- How will you develop these as part of your continual professional development?

Differences between management and leadership

Much debate exists relating to whether management and leadership are one and the same. Indeed, one might argue that individuals cannot be effective leaders nor managers without a sharing of the qualities identified in Figure 2.2. The Skills for Care report *Leadership and Management: A Strategy for the Social Care Workforce* (2006) argues that 'leadership and management are part of the same continuum rather than being separate activities'. Consider the qualities and behaviours identified below; where would you place yourself on the continuum between manager and leader?

Managers	Leaders
administrate	innovate
maintain	develop
engage systems/structures	focus on people
rely on control	inspire trust
keep an eye on the budget	look to the future

Figure 2.2   Manager–leader continuum

Summary

This chapter has considered the discipline of management and how this relates to the social care role. We have identified key features and reviewed the quasi-market in which the present day social care service operates. Planning and financial resources have been identified as key tasks both for the practitioner, the manager, the team and the organisation. We have finally posed the question as to whether management and leadership are part of the same continuum, and the same role, within the social care organisation. We will continue this debate further in later chapters.

CHAPTER 3

Managing and Leading in Different Environments

Key themes in this chapter include:
The internal and external environment
Stakeholders
SWOT Analysis
Managing multi-disciplinary teams
Managing transient staff
Leading the team

Introduction

As part of a management team, social work and social care managers will manage and work with colleagues throughout the organisation who may share a similar professional background. However, equally, social work and social care managers will manage teams made up of personnel from different disciplines or sit on management boards that include different professional groups, service users and carers or other stakeholders. Social work and social care practice and therefore management may be located within a statutory agency but, equally, may be delivered within a community setting, charitable, voluntary or private organisation.

From a team or organisation perspective, perhaps some staff are permanent members, perhaps some are short-term, temporary, members on fixed contracts within the team or organisation, engaged for specific tasks or projects, or perhaps some are so transient that it is not known how long they will remain, such as agency staff. Some teams or organisations may be together under the same roof whilst other teams may be virtual in that they may have little physical contact with each other on a day-to-day basis, such as workers who are based at home or in satellite offices many miles away from other team colleagues. Each member will have their own needs as an employee and worker, and bring with them their own level of expertise, knowledge base and expectations. The challenge for managers is to ensure that they come together as a collective and united whole who share the same vision, mission, goals, aims and objectives.

It has to be acknowledged, therefore, that the 'mix' of teams and organisations today does not mirror the stability that was once seen. On the whole, the workforce is more transient and workers do not stay in the same organisation or job throughout their working life as they once did. Organisations and teams today need, therefore, to be flexible and adaptable to the changing needs of workers alongside the similar changing needs of society, the local community and the consumer or client. The social care manager needs to understand and acknowledge the changing environment in which she or he operates whilst managing in a safe, competent, informed and professional manner. In the previous chapter we discussed leadership from a macro perspective, and here we will expand on this and also relate leadership to teams and individuals.

The Skills for Care/TOPPS report (2006: 7.2) clearly points out that:

> *The key purpose of management and leadership is to provide direction, gain commitment, facilitate change and achieve results through the efficient, creative and responsible deployment of people and other resources.*
>
> (Skills for Care/TOPPS, 2006)

The Government's Performance and Innovation Unit research study *Strengthening Leadership in the Public Sector: A Research Study by the PIU* (2001) points out that Britain's public services face unprecedented challenges within a rapidly changing environment which include:

- Demands to modernise public services and orient them more closely to the needs and wishes of customers.
- Higher expectations on the part of the general public, who expect public services to keep up with private ones.
- Increased opportunities, and requirements, for partnerships both across the public sector and with private and voluntary organisations.
- Pressures to harness new technology and deliver government services electronically.

Indeed the Performance and Innovation Unit report quotes Sir Richard Wilson, Cabinet Secretary, as stating that:

> *Public services in the past tended to be something which people got, not as a right but as a favour bestowed at the discretion of the State. Along with that went a tacit understanding that the service might be a bit shabby, slow and bureaucratic. But that was the price of getting something for free. The public were expected to accept that a public service would not be as good as something which you paid for. This is not how most people see it now. People expect from public services the standards which they would get from the private sector.*
>
> (PIU, 2001: 2.1, 11)

This chapter will consider some of the complexities that managers face within today's changing working environment and, with the aid of management tools and strategies, examples and activities, the following concepts will be explored:

- The near and far – internal and external environment in which managers operate.
- Stakeholders and interest groups.
- Managing the changing team.

The internal and external environment in which we work

Working in the public sector today brings with it many challenges as we have already shown. A great many of those challenges are a direct result of the rapid changes being felt within the public and voluntary sector. These changes are brought about by factors in both the internal environment and the external environment in which the public sector operates.

Initially, it is necessary to think about what we mean by the internal and external environment, how the internal and external environments co-exist and who the stakeholders are within that. Consider the figure below, which outlines the overlapping nature of the internal and external environment.

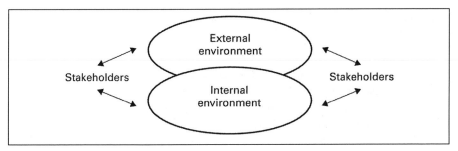

Figure 3.1

Depending on your level of responsibility within your organisation you may consider that your internal environment is one that includes your caseload or even a service user you are working with; a group of workers that you supervise; the team that you manage; the management team that you belong to or your organisation as a whole. Clearly, you may belong to several groupings within your internal environment in line with your differing levels of responsibility and these may then form the hierarchy of your professional demands.

Consider, for example, as shown in Figure 3.2, the internal environment of a team manager within a multi-disciplinary setting and just some of the groups of people who are likely to have a vested interest in what they do, as team manager, as part of their management role.

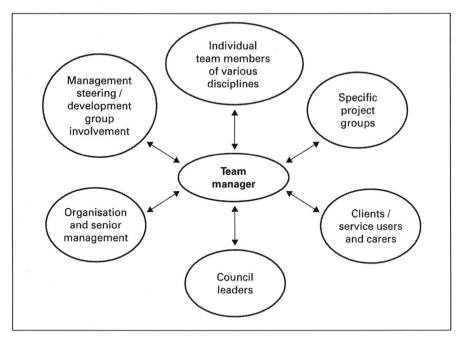

Figure 3.2

Activity 3.1

Think about the current internal environment for your role within your workplace. Your current internal environment may, in line with your specific role and responsibility, be interpreted as your organisation, your team, the group of workers that you manage or even your own managed caseload.

Complete your own internal environment diagram showing the people who are dependent on your role.

- Do all those people or groups receive or make equal demands on your time?
- Do all the individuals or groups identified share equal power when competing for your time, commitment and decision making capabilities?

The external environment is one which is outside your internal environment, although it does have an impact and influence on it. As Figure 3.1 shows there is a blurring of boundaries and overlap and connection between them. Because of their connectivity any change in either environment will have a subsequent change on the other. Let us consider some of the areas of influence of the same team manager's external environment:

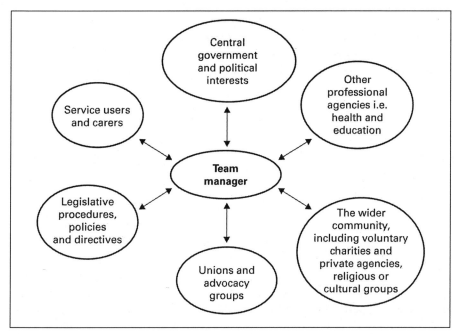

Figure 3.3

Activity 3.2
Consider and map the external environment which has an impact on how you operate. How important do you consider this external environment to be on your day-to-day work practice?

Stakeholders

The internal and external environment in which you operate will include a range of different stakeholders with differing needs. A stakeholder can be seen as an individual, a group of individuals, organisations or other groupings which have a vested interest in what is going on within their internal or external environment. Indeed, Johnson and Scholes (1999: 213) remind us that:

Stakeholders are those individuals or groups who depend on the organisation to fulfil their own goals and to whom, in turn, the organisation depends.

It is likely that you will have identified different stakeholders within your internal and external environments. You might be wondering why it is important to identify them. Stakeholders can have a powerful influence on your team or organisation, particularly during times of change or if a manager wishes to implement change.

Johnson and Scholes (2001: 167) (in Mendelow, A. Proceedings of 2nd International Conference on Information Systems. Cambridge, MA, 1991) offer a very useful way of looking at mapping stakeholder interest using the dimensions of power and interest in the form of a matrix diagram:

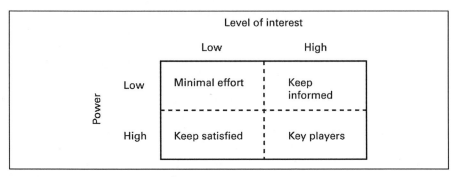

Figure 3.4

We can see that there are four distinct cells that can inform us of the importance of particular stakeholders based on the level of interest that a stakeholder might have and the power that they can exert. For example, if we feel that a change we are considering implementing is of high interest to a particular stakeholder but that stakeholder has little power over the proposed change, we might feel that it is important to keep them informed but little else is necessary at this time. However, if we considered that the stakeholder had a high degree of interest and also had a significantly high level of power over a proposed change, positive or negative, then clearly they are highly important to the successful implementation and are so considered to be key players. Taking important stakeholders 'along with you' on the journey of change is, therefore, crucial in order that they can share with the vision, make an input into that vision and feel part of the process.

Activity 3.3

You are the manager of a multi-professional team. Your organisation has asked you to produce a report on the impact of the proposed closure of a local day centre that is used by many service users and carers in the area. Clearly, this change might have a significant impact on those who attend, and you might have ethical reservations and considerations about undertaking this task. However, there is also likely to be a significant impact for other stakeholders in both the internal and external environments in which you operate.

Using your skills of identifying the internal and external environment in which you work as outlined in Activity 3.2 and 3.3, consider the stakeholder mapping grid outlined in Figure 3.4 and plot the level of power and interest of the identified stakeholders. You may wish to complete one map for the internal environment and another for the external environment.

- How useful are these maps in identifying where and who you should collaborate with about this proposed change?
- Will the changes affect the internal and external stakeholders in the same way?
- In your role as a social work or social care manager do you consider the internal or the external stakeholders interests as equally important?
- Does this raise dilemmas for you in your management role?
- How can you include stakeholders so that they feel part of the process?

SWOT analysis

Another way of considering the above scenario is to use a SWOT analysis (Coulshed et al., 2006; Gill, 2006; Have et al., 2003; Johnson and Scholes, 1999). SWOT analysis has primarily been discussed within private sector organisations as a strategic tool used to consider internal capabilities within the organisation in the form of strengths and weaknesses. It can also be used to respond to what is happening within the external environment that may hold opportunities and threats to the organisation from competitors vying for the same market. Clearly, for a private organisation, the focus is on gaining profit and sustainability as a result of capturing the consumers buying power from other organisations.

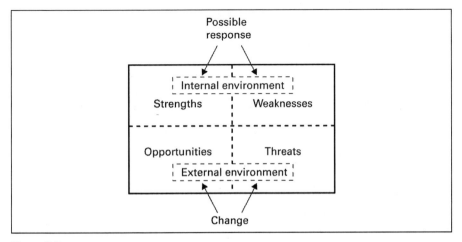

Figure 3.5

Adapting this model to a public sector or non-profit making organisation allows it to be used in a micro and practical sphere of decision making as well as a more macro strategic tool. We might consider this, for example, in relation to the quality of service being delivered and service user satisfaction or resources available. Westhues et al. (2001) used a SWOT analysis as part of their research when considering the human resource needs of social workers in Canada. By using this model, they concluded that:

Our review of the weaknesses and threats to the social work profession in Canada shows the profession to be experiencing an identity crisis and unable to articulate the contributions of social workers in promoting the well-being of society.

Activity 3.4

You manage a service area within a community based voluntary agency whose core business is working with and supporting adults in the community who have learning difficulties in order that they can remain within their own home. This is a locally based organisation and the staff group know the local community and resources well. The staff group are stable and have built up strong trusting relationships with service users over a long period. Your Director has advised you that it is likely that external funding for your organisation from statutory agencies is to be severely cut this coming financial year. You are asked to produce a balanced report for your Director outlining how proposed financial cuts could affect the service that you offer. You feel that a SWOT analysis might be useful, along with a stakeholder analysis, in logically outlining the impact on these changes.

- Outline who the likely stakeholders might be.
- Outline the power and influence the respective stakeholders might have on the proposed change.
- Undertake a SWOT analysis from the perspective of your organisation and then from the perspective of the service user.

Returning to our scenario, clearly one of the weaknesses of closing a day centre might be that service users and carers are left without a resource and, as such, their needs will not be met. We might argue that the quality of care will be diminished. However, from an organisation and management perspective the strength of such a change might be that this will free up scarce resources and finances which can be re-directed towards a more robust service, perhaps a multi-agency approach to meeting service users needs. Clearly, those multi-agency stakeholders are part of our external environment and we might consider that this is an opportunity for joint planning and working towards a more systematic community development. However, our analysis could indicate that a threat might be that our possible collaborators do not have the funds or do not see a new resource as a priority. A further threat might also arise from advocacy groups, service users and carers and other political actors who might fear that they could be left without a service.

A SWOT analysis is a useful management tool in that it gives a clear framework in which to formulate thinking about the impact of changes in the internal and external environment. As Gill reminds us (2006: 194) this then allows us to choose a strategy that will capitalise on the organisation's strengths, control its weaknesses, neutralise threats and exploit its opportunities (Barney, 1997). However, as Have et al. argue (2003: 188):

> *The problem is that the elements (SWOT) appear deceptively simple. Actually deciding what the strengths and weaknesses of your organisation are, as well as assessing the impact and probability of opportunities and threats, is far more complex than at first sight.*

STEEP analysis

In March 1999, the Government's Strategy Performance and Innovation Unit examined six key drivers of change and their impact for the future. This resulted in the report, *The Future and How to Think About It.* The six drivers of change listed below offer an additional and more specific dimension to those in Chapter 1:

- demographics
- science and technology
- environment
- attitudes and values
- economic globalisation
- political institutions

These macro drivers of change have a significant impact on the external environment and as such also within a social work and social care setting and, as noted earlier, therefore, have an impact on our internal environment of practice.

STEEP analysis (sometimes referred to as PEST analysis or PESTLE model) (Gill, 2006) is a useful tool to consider when looking at changes in the external environment and how future planning within the internal environment can meet changing needs:

- social
- technical
- environmental
- economic
- political

As social workers, social care workers and managers, we acknowledge that we work in a world which is constantly changing. From a macro perspective we know that our social environment is in constant demographic change. For example, people are living longer and teenage pregnancy is still rising within the UK which again results in a larger specific population with specific needs; our communities have a more diverse cultural composition which again presents specific needs. From an environmental perspective, there may be a corresponding need to plan both short term and long term resource allocation to meet the need by providing, for example, greater housing stock of affordable homes, schools, hospitals and nursing homes. Technically, it may be possible to provide the resources that are necessary. However, from an economic perspective, there are only finite resources to meet the needs as demand outstrips supply. Therefore, the targeting of finances and resources becomes necessary and decisions are needed in relation to prioritisation. How this is achieved is directed from the political stakeholder of those in power. These governmental directives inform the policies and procedures that subsequently inform practice.

> ### Activity 3.5
> As part of your management responsibilities you have been asked to look at how your organisation can plan and target resources for the current and future needs of your local community. Using the STEEP headings identified, map some of the drivers of change within the external environment and comment on how these changes might impact on your future provision and service?

To summarise this section, we have seen that managers have to manage complex external and internal working environments whilst ensuring that the core tasks and responsibilities of teams and organisations run efficiently, effectively and safely. This can and does present significant challenges for the public sector manager who has to reconcile the internal complexities of their teams with the demands from external change, pressures and demands. We might say, as managers, that if we managed the ideal team or organisation – where the workforce was stable and had worked together for a long period of time; where everyone had the same knowledge base and level of expertise; where everyone was highly motivated and shared similar values and practised using the same professional codes of practice – this might be straightforward. However, we know that teams are generally not like that and as a result the social work and social care team or organisation of today offers the social care manager many challenges.

Managing multi disciplinary teams

As the Skills for Care/TOPPS report *Leadership Management: A Strategy for the Social Care Workforce* (2006: 7.4) states:

It is vital that leadership and management standards capture the importance of leading and managing complexity and diversity; this may be across agencies, in integrated services and through contracts. Any leadership and management standards/competences framework should promote:
- *Flexible career pathways across integrated services.*
- *Transferable skills across agencies.*
- *Applicability to diverse organisations and individuals.*

Activity 3.6

Think about an activity that you have been involved in which has necessitated working with and alongside other people. Perhaps you have belonged to a sports team or a member of a group of people organising an event. As part of the team you may have found that you have worked together for a common goal or outcome.

Was your team successful and if so why? Think about why it was perhaps not so successful and list reasons for this.

Perhaps you listed things like being able to communicate well together; everyone knowing their collective and own roles within the group/team; everyone knowing what the desired outcome was; being able to understand the rules of the game; supporting other team members if they were injured or feeling below par; being able to step into each others role if necessary; knowing the culture of the team; being able to bond together by the commonality of sharing past stories and myths; knowing the unspoken rules.

As Øvretveit (1997: 9) states:

We have all joined a team, only to discover it was not the type of team which we imagined. We remember that team members emphasised how good and close the teamwork was, but said little more. The operational policy seemed to explain it all, but after a while we saw the gaps in the policy and noticed that people do not follow it. They all did their own thing, and some did not even come to the team meetings. In fact, many seemed to be members of other teams. Should we start asking questions, or start to contribute to 'the myth of the team'? Perhaps, in time, we will learn to see the emperor's clothes.

For the social care manager, the task of managing teams which consist of professional workers from different disciplines can present many challenges but also many rewards, particularly for the service user. As we know, people do not encounter 'stand alone' problems. There may be a primary cause of a problem but the effect will ripple out into other areas of a person's life or the lives of those around them. As a consequence there may be many professional people involved – constituting a professional network.

As Barrett et al. remind us (2005: 1) the nature of health and social care is such that, for many, the quality of service received is dependant upon how effectively different professional groups work together. Indeed, Irvine et al. (2002: 208) argue that professionals have a moral obligation to work together to ensure that service users' interests are paramount.

Within the current literature, there are many terms to describe the coming together of different professional groups in the course of their work with service users. For example, inter-agency working can be described as that which involves colleagues from other professional groups i.e. education, health, housing, who may work within their respective teams but may also work with colleagues from other teams at particular times when the need of the service user warrants it. Multi-disciplinary working also refers to work with colleagues from other disciplines but those colleagues may physically sit together within formally formed multi-disciplinary teams. Quinney (2006: 13) outlines the 'lexicon of terms' that are commonly used – inter-agency working, inter-disciplinary working, multi-agency working, multi-professional working, uni-professional working, inter-professional working, partnership working, working together. However, to clarify we might say that it is the beliefs, values and actions arising from working with other professional colleagues that are important and what we call it is of less significance. Indeed, Whittington (2003: 16) offers the following:

Partnership is a state of relationships, at organisational, group, professional or inter-professional level, to be achieved, maintained and reviewed; and collaboration is the active process of partnership in action.

Consider an ideal type model typical of professional groups who may form part of an inter-professional team. You will note that the service user is at the centre of the team.

Activity 3.7
Using Figure 3.6 as a model, think about the team or organisation that you currently manage and the professional diversity of the team.

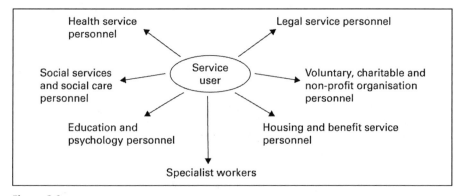

Figure 3.6

The team may physically be together or virtual. Identify the potential strengths of the diversity of your team for the different stake-holders that you identified earlier – particularly for the service user or carer.

Let us consider more specifically the complexity of this for managers in relation to specific duties and responsibilities. We will also consider why effective management of multi-professional teams is vital.

Figure 3.7 outlines some of the responsibilities and considerations of a social care manager within a multi-professional team.

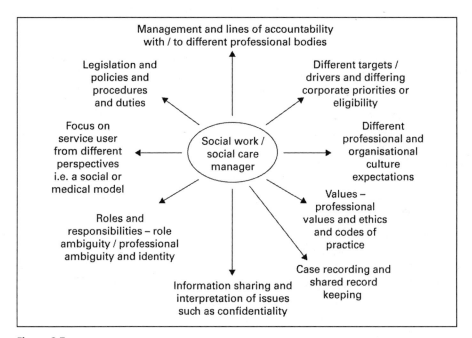

Figure 3.7

From a practice perspective, it is well argued that, generally, the management of elements of the above diagram have historically not been robust and the service provided has failed service users and carers and, indeed, employees. The Chief Government Inspector, Denise Platt CBE (2001) in her review of research on the Children Act 1989, wrote of the need for an effective, integrated children care planning and assessment system, better management information and competent professional staff.

The Department of Health document *Working Together to Safeguard Children* (1999) states:

Promoting children's well-being and safeguarding them from significant harm depends crucially upon effective information sharing, collaboration and understanding between agencies and professionals.

Lord Laming's report into the death of Victoria Climbié, and the subsequent Green Paper *Every Child Matters* (2003: 21) expanded on the above by stating:

Our existing system for supporting children and young people who are beginning to experience difficulties is often poorly co-ordinated and account-ability is unclear. This means that information is not shared between agencies so that warning signs are not recognised and acted upon. Some children are assessed many times by different agencies and despite this may get no services. Children may experience a range of professionals involved in their lives but little continuity and consistency of support. Organisations may disagree over who should pay for meeting children's needs because their problems cut across organisational boundaries.

The Children Act (2004: 6, 1) states:

Each children's services authority in England must make arrangements to promote co-operation between:
(a) the authority
(b) each of the authority's relevant partners; and
(c) such other persons or bodies as the authority consider appropriate, being persons or bodies of any nature who exercise functions or are engaged in activities in relation to children in the authority's area.

The National Service Framework for Older People, *Modern Standards and Service Models* (2001) also reiterates:

The Health Act 1999 places a duty of partnership on health authorities and councils which is reflected in Health Improvement Programmes. The Local Government Act 2000 provides additional powers for councils to work in partnership with other local agencies to improve economic, social and environmental well-being.

Inclusive planning is highlighted on page 117:

The NSF implementation arrangements will bring together all the health, social services and housing agencies involved, as well as the independent sector and wider partners, including other elements of the local council. Older people, reflecting the diversity of communities, and their carers and their representa-tives should also be included.

The *Single Assessment Process – Older People: Guidance and Annexes* (2002) outlines joint working arrangements in relation to the assessment process:

Where specialist assessments are called for, possibly culminating in a comprehensive assessment, a range of qualified professionals and specialists could be involved, including: social workers, nurses, occupational therapists, physiotherapists, speech and language therapists, dieticians, podiatrists, dentists and dental hygienists, physicians, geriatricians, old age psychiatrists, other consultants working with older people, and professionals from other agencies including housing . . . they should seek to promote responsible team working and flexibility.

These statements indicate strong messages from Central Government and therefore should reflect the way that direct work with service users is managed and implemented locally. Clearly, the social work and social care manager needs to be able to identify barriers that might stand in the way of effective multi-professional working and initiate plans to break down possible barriers.

A research study conducted by Northumberland Council (2003) (http:www.northumberland.gov.uk), in response to the Children's National Service Framework, asked professionals who worked in multi-agency teams what they saw as the barriers and solutions to multi-agency working.

The solutions they identified included:

- Getting people around the table – which may mean well planned meetings.
- Sharing knowledge about each others' roles and targets. Having respect for each others' roles and professional skills and abilities.
- Having trust for colleagues' judgements.
- Working in environments together to develop relationships.
- Standardising protocols.
- Believing that multi-agency work is important – being motivated and overcoming difficulties.

Molyneux (2001) in her research study explored how and why co-operative and positive working relationships and practice developed within one inter-professional health care team in the North East of England. She concluded that success was gained through:

- Appointing motivated, committed and experienced staff.
- Staff who were flexible in their working relationships and working practices.
- Staff who demonstrated flexibility and adaptability which allowed team members to work across professional boundaries.
- Staff who were confident in their professional role which came with a long experience of working in their own field.

Activity 3.8

You currently manage a team of social workers who work with adults with physical and sensory difficulties. Re-organisation has necessitated the joining up with other teams from a health discipline and you will now manage a team which consists of social workers, occupational therapists and district nurses. Using the management diagrams outlined in this chapter what difficulties do you feel might emerge and what solutions can you immediately put into place to ensure that the team functions as a whole and the service users' needs are not compromised.

The management of transient staff

As we have discussed above, the key to success, which equates with providing the best possible care and support for service users, is found within teams themselves and how they are managed. However, the committed, motivated, knowledgeable team needs time, consistency and stability to evolve and grow. This is something which has been lacking within the social care and public sector arena. Indeed, demand for qualified social workers and social care workers still exceeds supply.

The Prime Minister, Tony Blair, speaking on modernising public services on 26th January 1999 (Audit Commission, 2002) comments:

There was a time when we could assume that the brightest and best of each generation would want to join the public sector. But that is an assumption that we can no longer make, particularly when the financial rewards at the top of the private sector are so great, and too often public sector workers are weighed down by bureaucracy and silly rules.

The proportion of the workforce employed by the public sector is falling. In 1981 public sector employees made up nearly 30 per cent of the UK workforce. This proportion has fallen to under 20 per cent in 2001 (*Economic Trends No. 583*, June 2002). Trends suggest that fewer people are directly employed by a public sector employer even though the number of people providing public services has increased along with demand. Many public sector social care providers have, over recent years, sought to fill their vacancies by using a transient workforce of short term agency staff. This clearly has significant and adverse implications for already overstretched budgets.

Indeed, as Ward et al. argue (2001: 4) within the present labour market a third of new engagements are accounted for by temporary jobs, a large proportion of which take the form of placements through temporary work agencies. Ward further argues that although the exact number of temporary agency employees has grown significantly over the last ten years, in some workplaces workers recruited through temporary work agencies may even have become the 'core', not just in the sense that they are quantitatively larger than the permanent workforce, but also in that their presence at the workplace determines its culture and dynamics.

This is no more apparent than within the social care sector and can be seen as a direct result of the gap between the supply and demand of the external labour market which includes changing demographic features of those who wish to undertake social work training. Batty (2002: 2) states that, between 1995 and 2001, there was a 59 per cent decrease in the numbers of students applying to undertake the two year social work diploma. Much now rests on the recently introduced three year degree programme to turn this around (Hayes, 2003). However, these factors obviously have an impact on future planning for the whole profession. Indeed, Prasad (2001) argues:

Lack of effective workforce planning leads to a vicious cycle of heavy workloads, long hours, low morale and high staff turnover.

For a team or organisation manager the dilemma is one of not only acting as an interpreter of corporate policy for transient staff but also imparting this knowledge to an occupationally and contractually divided workforce. For a manager in a social care department where the work is very complex and embedded within organisational culture, legislation and bureaucracy which can often involve life changing decision making, there may be many knowledge gaps leading to the potential for wrong or ill informed decisions which can then result in serious consequences. Indeed, the very nature of social work practice is based on the need for good communication and the sharing of knowledge and trust between the manager and the social worker. This is built up over time, something unfortunately that the manager and the transient worker do not have. In a research study conducted by Williams and Young (2003) team managers were asked to comment on the difficulties in managing transient teams. One manager is quoted as saying:

On the one hand it is more difficult because there is no such thing now as a stable and fully staffed team made up of permanent workers, but, at the same time the actual work has become much more complex with a lot of procedures for which you need a stable team to impart the knowledge about the new procedures.

Indeed, the Victoria Climbié Inquiry (Lord Laming, 2003: para 1.56/7) identifies significant child protection risks associated with the widespread employment of qualified social work agency staff:

The practice of using a front-line 'duty team' with agency staff is totally unacceptable.

Ward et al. (2001: 17) argued that the performance of the team and department was unlikely to be enhanced by the use of large numbers of temporary agency workers and also, the extensive use of agency workers was not sustainable for anything more than a short period of time. However, local authorities, it seems, have no option but to 'take on' agency staff in order that they can attempt to meet the demands of their various stakeholders. The team manager is responsible for not only managing governmental change through policy and organisational change through procedure, but also has to interpret and impart continuous and copious new initiatives and knowledge to a transient team of workers, perhaps from different professional backgrounds, in order that they can work in a local community in such a way as to ensure that a safe and quality driven service is maintained.

As such, a team manager's responsibility within the social care sector of the 21st century is many faceted and one which carries with it a significant role as a pivotal driver of change throughout the whole organisation. Indeed, Dobson and Stewart's (cited in Mabey et al., 1993: 43) study of the role of middle managers showed a need for:

> . . . *greater flexibility and adaptability . . . more generalist skills which included financial knowledge, a greater ability to manage staff and staff of different backgrounds, a wider understanding of what is happening around them both in other departments and outside, and a greater marketing and strategic operation.*

Leading the successful team

Organisations, be they public or private or 'not for profit' need to function efficiently and effectively. The sum of an organisation is greater than its parts. Human resources, in the form of employees, are a significant part, along with the technology, and other extrinsic resources. An organisation will run into difficulties if it is a production firm and its machinery stops working. Similarly, a service sector organisation cannot function and provide a service if the people who provide that service are not willing or able to do their job.

Leadership, as we have argued previously, has for some time been identified as a key determinant of the success of organisations. Research suggests that creating the appropriate climate within a team can account for approximately 30 per cent of the variation in its performance and that the leader has a critical influence on this climate. About 70 per cent of organisational climate is influenced by the styles, or consistent patterns of behaviour, a leader deploys in relating to others within the team.

The General Social Care Council *Specialist Standards and Requirements for Post-qualifying Social Work Education and Training* argue (2005: 3) that the quality of professional leadership and management is of vital importance to users of social care services. Sue Mead, Audit Commission Director of Joint Reviews (2004) states:

> *The quality of leadership and management are the key factors driving improvement. What works best is a business-like approach underpinned by the values of social care and an understanding of why it matters to communities.*

Leading the team

Current literature and research suggests that there are three key theoretical approaches to defining leadership – trait, style, contingency. We have touched on these previously but will expand further by relating these to task and people.

Trait theories of leadership have their origins in the early part of the 20th century alongside the growth of psychometric assessment procedures. Today, these are still favoured for recruitment into senior positions in organisations, particularly where organisations outsource their recruitment to specialist recruitment consultants. Advocates for this form of selection suggest that there are personality and person qualities which are essential for leadership roles, such as, intelligence, self-confidence, assertiveness. This implies that people are either born with or acquire through socialisation the necessary traits (Kotter, 1990: 106).

Style theories suggest, however, that it is not the psychological characteristics of people that are important, but, rather, how they behave – the style of leadership that they adopt.

Blake and Mouton (1962) identified within their study two polar types of leader –

- Those concerned with task (getting the task done).
- Those concerned with people (concerned with working relationships).

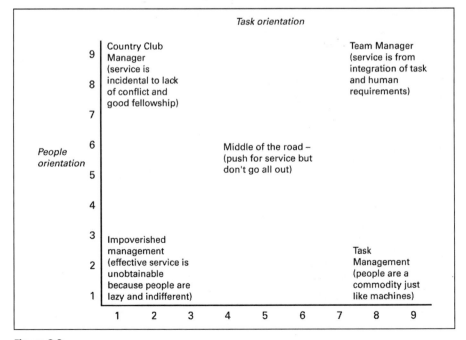

Figure 3.8

We can see from the above that the most optimum managerial style might be that of 'team manager' where there is a high and equal concern for the task but also for the team members who are able to complete what is asked of them.

Contingency theories go one step further by challenging the view that there is one best theory. They argue that the best form of leadership depends on the situation. This denotes a further quality of flexibility and adaptability.

> **Activity 3.9**
> Consider Blake and Mouton's grid and determine the following:
> - Think about a team in which you have worked in the past. Where would you place your manager or a manager you have known on this grid?
> - Do you think this is the best place to be on the grid? Give reasons.
> - Where are you and where would you wish to be on the grid and give reasons why?

Instead of thinking about leadership as the characteristics or style of a person with authority (as we have seen above) another view is seeing it as an influencing process. We can say that this form of leadership involves 'taking people with you'.

Leadership has some important common features across all sectors, but it must also be adapted to the distinctive context of public services. As we have noted, public services are highly diverse and operate within a political context where accountability and funding are significant issues. It is argued that leadership within the public sector should reflect these unique requirements and that effective leadership should:

- Not rely on personal characteristics such as charisma alone but further be based on the ability to motivate others towards best outcomes and practice.
- Possess the organisational skills that recognise the complexity of the modern organisation and focus on defining and communicating mission and strategy rather than issuing commands.
- Possess the ability to work well with other organisations to define and achieve common goals.

The NHS *Leadership Qualities Framework* (2002: 15) provides us with a very useful model which firmly places an individual's personal qualities at the centre.

As we can see from Figure 3.9, two clearly defined roles are identified – setting direction and delivering the service. Setting direction includes intellectual flexibility, a drive for results, political astuteness, broad scanning and seizing the future. Delivering the service includes leading change through people, holding to account, empowering others, effective and strategic influencing, collaborative working.

In later chapters we will discuss the crucial role that motivation plays in both setting direction and in delivering the service.

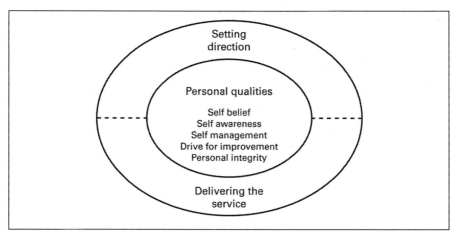

Figure 3.9

Summary

This chapter has looked at change through managing and leading. We have discussed the complexities that the current social work and social care manager faces from the internal and external environment and identified the stakeholders that may have power and influence on the management role. Several management tools have been presented which can practically assist the management task when faced with difficult decisions and competing demands. We have considered why effective management is necessary and have firmly placed the service user at the heart of what we do and why we do it.

CHAPTER 4

The Influence of Policy

> **Key themes in this chapter include:**
> Policy and processes
> Legislation
> Policy as a coping mechanism
> Policy and values
> The learning organisation

What is policy?

At first you may wonder what policy has to do with your role as a social worker. The answer is a great deal. Much of what we do as a manager or social worker is influenced by policy and procedure yet policy is difficult to define because its meaning is hotly contested. There are, however, a number of essential characteristics of policy that help us to understand its importance and influence on organisational activities and practice. The first is that policy is developed within a framework of objectives and guidelines for action and for this reason we find policy relating to all activities of the organisation. At a strategic level and within client group specialisms, policy statements set out service aims and aspirations and describe the values, beliefs and principles that underpin the organisations' activities.

In addition to reinforcing its main functions, policy clarifies the roles and responsibilities of social workers and other members of staff. It makes for consistency in decision-making and reduces dependency on the actions of individual managers. In all these areas policy provides direction and is a means of seeking to ensure that standards and practice do not fall below an acceptable level. From this we can see that policy is also a means of control that influences what social workers and managers do, how they behave, the provision of services and allocation of resources.

Activity 4.1
Some voluntary and independent organisations have very few policies compared with organisations in the statutory sector. If very few policies exist what impact might this have for:
- the organisation
- social care workers

- service users
- other stakeholders

The legal context

The law applies to all aspects of an organisation and many aspects of law will impinge on the social work role. As such it is wide ranging and gives authorities duties, responsibilities and powers to provide services and make decisions as to whether people are eligible to receive a service. The law gives authorities powers to intervene in people's lives, for example, child protection, as well as identifying those groups entitled to services such as children in need (Children Act, 1989) and adults who have been detained in hospital (Mental Health Act, 1983). There are laws relating to confidentiality, data protection, human rights and employment, including health and safety legislation and anti-discriminatory practice.

Legislation underpins the performance of the professional task and, in this respect, the law is often specific and explicit about what can and cannot be done. On the other hand there is considerable scope for interpretation of law and this can apply at four main levels:

1. *Statutory guidance* issued through government departments on how legislation should be applied.
2. *Local policies and procedures* developed by local authorities and other social work agencies in line with their interpretation of the law and its requirements.
3. *Precedent* set by the courts in specific cases which forms the baseline from which future decisions will be made.
4. *Professional practice* and discretion is a further stage of interpretation because the law does not dictate precisely how a social worker should act in all situations.

(Thompson, 2005: 36)

It would not be unusual to hear social workers and managers complain that they feel weighed down by organisational policies and procedures, yet it is difficult to imagine the effectiveness of a 'policyless' organisation anymore than one could accept the notion of 'theoryless' practice.

Being knowledgeable about the law, government guidance, and regulation documents is essential for competent practice but there are government, departmental and inspection publications that social workers and managers need to keep pace with as well, as they are directly relevant to their work. Social workers have the additional responsibility of gaining knowledge of the agency's structure, how it is managed and how the individual worker fits within the organisation's policy and procedures relevant to their roles and responsibilities. As a social worker bidding for finite resources, you may not always be successful, after all organisations cannot allocate resources they do not have, but linking assessed need with organisational policy makes the bid very much more powerful. This is because an organisation cannot deny its own policy and has to accept ownership if shortfalls in resources lead to assessed need not being met. This responsibility sits with the organisation and not the social worker.

Practitioners may not routinely be referring to any formal sources of law in carrying out their professional tasks but instead will make reference to the organisation's policy and procedures manual. It is, however, important to remember that an organisation's internal policies are only valid to the extent that they accord with an accurate interpretation of statute, regulation or guidance. Generally, social workers need to know about the law because it tells them what their powers and duties are. A power, for example, is granted to an organisation or individual to provide a certain service, but they do not necessarily have to do so. Duty, on the other hand, is something the organisation or individual has to carry out and is therefore a '*must*'. The law also sets lines of accountability and ensures that the process of decision making is fair and equitable. The law cannot resolve the everyday dilemmas of social work practice, neither can it tell social workers what to do in every situation: it can only set out the framework.

Activity 4.2
Identify a piece of legislation that you currently work with. Identify your lines of accountability and how this impacts on your professional relationship with service users and carers:
- Where does the power lie?
- How does this influence your practice as a manager?

Activity 4.3
You are a team manager in a very busy frontline children and families team. Your senior manager has advised you that the expectation for completing initial assessments (7 days) needs to be raised. As a manager you have to consider how you can raise this figure within your team whilst also considering your staff group who you know are working as hard as they can. In order to implement this policy you have to grapple with the feelings that you personally may have about the policy, the feelings of your team when you tell them to work harder or differently, the feelings of your senior manager and the organisation if you can't make the shift that they want.
- How can you satisfy everyone?
- How would you try?
- How would you feel?

Who makes policy?
To this question there is no simple answer, but includes a web of different interests, influences and individuals, all of whom, over time, exert influence on

policy. That is not to suggest that the process is evenly weighted, since experience points to some groups being capable of exerting greater impact on public opinion than others. Since policies are guidelines for making executive decisions and determining action, policy making must be mindful of the type of action and decisions that will be required under a given set of circumstances and conditions. Policy making cannot therefore be divorced from significant events. Following the inquiry into the death of Victoria Cimbié (2003) for example, there have been initiatives through the Children Act 2004 and *Every Child Matters* (2004) introducing important changes to social work practice with children and their families. While public opinion was not the major driving force behind these changes there continues to be a need to address public confidence in the capacity of social work, as a profession, to assure the welfare of vulnerable children. Public perception is, therefore, an important consideration in setting policy objectives.

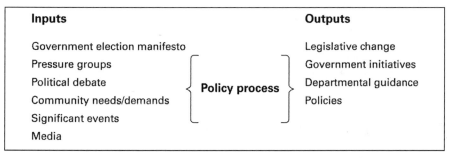

Figure 4.1

Local authorities are charged with responsibilities for implementing a range of centrally determined policies with central government more prescriptive than ever before in setting out what is expected and how money should be spent. As such, the roles of a local authority have been curtailed. Given that approximately 70 per cent of a local authority's income comes from central government, the powerful influence over local authority service provision is clear. The introduction of the modernisation agenda is an example of a central government initiative aimed at reducing local government's political control of social services. Whether these changes make those services more responsive to the needs of people or constitute a step towards privatisation and erosion of local democracy is an important debate. The example of private finance initiatives in health and education offers an insight into the current trend that may increasingly engage social care.

As a planning activity, policy must be as objective as possible, involving the collection and assessment of factual information but, as we discussed previously, the complex and unpredictable nature of social care makes this a difficult task.

The future policy implications, nevertheless, assume even greater importance in a climate of rapid changes in structure, location and practice in social care provision. It is an opportunity to think about what services could be like.

Activity 4.4
- Identify three policies that you currently work with. Identify the principles that underpin these policies.
- What do they convey to you about the purpose and aims of the organisation.
- What might differentiate the policies of public, private and independent sector organisations.

Policy as a coping mechanism

Policy makers can make policies, but it is far more difficult to ensure that these policies are implemented and that they achieve the desired results. It is rarely the policy makers who really determine policy but social workers and other staff working face-to-face with service users. Consider the following:

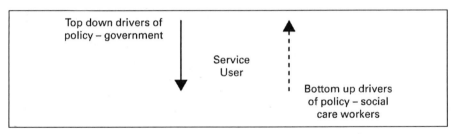

Figure 4.2

Social workers are not just struggling with a new language of resource management and with the business of setting up contracts (Leat and Perkins, 1998) but they do this in a context dictated by scarcity of resources, demanding and tight control of budgets, strict eligibility, high caseloads and maximum outputs (Dustin, 2000). Some policy initiatives are enabling in that they provide opportunity for service users to participate in assessment, service design and delivery. Government on the other hand can, through funding policies, reduce both the range and quality of service which public and independent agencies can provide. Too often in these circumstances practice becomes budgetary – rather than needs – led.

Coping mechanisms, such as eligibility criteria, targeting and greatest needs policies are designed to ration inadequate resources in the face of growing demand and budgetary shortfalls. A relatively static resource base has meant a shift from front line services towards management and regulation, through policies of control that represent ways of making it appear at the strategic level that the local authority is coping (Wolstenholme et al., 2006). Institutionalising the coping policies can have serious implications for the morale of staff who see the realisation of the apparent incapacity of social care systems to offer any kind of service stability to the most troubled, damaged and vulnerable members of the community. It is interesting that some coping policies are now regarded as formal policies despite corporate objectives that create expectations of choice, needs-led and client-centred services. Such apparent contradictions have led some critics to conclude that mission statements lack substance and serve only to confuse colleagues and service users alike (Trapp, 1999). Indeed, so much is asked of social work today that it would probably be impossible to live up to the expectations of the public through the issuing of well intended service aspirations. The concern is that coping policies lead to assessed need being measured not in terms of human experience but organisationally determined and with priorities aimed at addressing budgetary pressures.

Despite the many difficulties, local authorities have to be seen to meet demand for their services and, when resources are limited, the way in which policies and procedures are followed becomes important in the allocation of resources. An authority cannot set eligibility criteria so high that obviously the most vulnerable people are excluded. They have also to manage the consequence of coping strategies that succeed in holding back demand while creating cumulative unmet need with future higher cost implications for social and health care organisations. While rationing services remains a well-established strategy to cope with resource imbalances, delaying intervention can, in many cases, accelerate deterioration in already difficult individual and family circumstances. Furthermore, it places still further distance between this and the legal and professional imperative for preventative and rehabilitative social work. Although these services may increasingly fall within the remit of other agencies, social workers and managers will continue to have a pivotal role to play in balancing and responding to the potentially conflicting needs of their agency, the government and service users.

The context of service demand is complex and the coping mechanisms described are well intentioned policies aimed at controlling finite budgets. They are, on the other hand, short- term 'fixes' that can dominate professional activity and challenge the beliefs and values that form the foundation of professional practice.

Activity 4.5
Within existing resources you have been asked to re-allocate your organisations' budget between services:
- Identify the principles that will inform your decision making.
- How will conflicting priorities between services be resolved.
- Draw up a list of potential savings you would want to make to reinvest in services.

Tensions between policy and practice

It has long been recognised that values have an important part to play in shaping policy especially where traditional values have been made explicit as a basis for practice (Thompson, 2005). The work of Biestek (1961), for example, has been influential in developing principles of acceptance, ventilation (expression of feelings), self-determination, non-judgementalism and confidentiality, all of which form an integral part of the practice value base. Emphasis on the innate worth and value of an individual is the ingredient that makes it possible to establish the relationship of trust that is essential for working with service users. Consequently, values are an important influence on actions and attitudes – they will encourage us to do certain things and not do others.

Values are a strong force in shaping peoples' behaviour and responses, particularly in situations which give rise to conflicts and tensions between personal commitment to meeting unmet need and organisational objectives to control expenditure. One of the possible consequences is for staff to become 'functionaries', to lose their compassion in a web of bureaucratic routines, procedures and standard practice (Thompson, 2005). The challenge, Thompson suggests, is to maintain a compassionate and humanitarian approach in the face of pressures to conform to organisational requirements and expectations.

Some commentators have viewed this as a moment of demoralisation in which staff become 'alienated from the environment and no longer able to be creative and flexible' (Clough, 1998: 88). As Sapey (2002) observes, social workers work in organisational structures which devalue direct work with service users.

> Activity 4.6
> Undertake an analysis of your organisation's policies:
> - How many emphasise the importance of direct work with service users by outlining tasks or practice?
> - How many outline the importance of administrative tasks?

In busy social care organisations the time to stop and think about the wider purpose can easily become taken up in activities of survival, and the strong links between purpose, policy, values and behaviour can be weakened. The most powerful source of a sense of purpose is the link between behaviours, the organisation's values and those underpinning professional practice. Social workers are motivated to work more creatively if they believe in what they are doing and trust the organisation they are working with. If policies, standards and behaviour can be justified in terms of values, they have a meaning for practitioners. If social workers are unable to identify with the values enshrined in the organisation's policies then they are arguably less likely to feel a sense of purpose about the activity. In the absence of a shared purpose, loyalty and commitment to the organisation becomes weakened and organisational objectives more difficult to achieve. Where there is a shared sense of purpose people find it easier to work together in search of new approaches to problem solving, starting with the question 'what is *jointly* expected of us?'

Becoming a 'learning organisation' (Senge, 1990) implies gathering the practice experience, wisdom and skills across all levels of staff within the organisation. The value of these contributions should not be underestimated. While tensions and dilemmas created by the infinite nature of need are an inevitability for social care organisations, coping strategies informed by the 'swampy lowlands' of practice (Schon, 1987) and less by the heights of political expediency, offer the potential for a more practice-based alternative. Policy formation should not be seen as synonymous with the role of senior management.

Activity 4.7
Draw up a list of the ways in which practice experience in your organisation can be used to inform policy development.
- Say how policies might change as a consequence.
- Would your organisation listen and act on messages from the 'bottom'?

As we have seen, demand and resources are central drivers in the introduction of coping policies but they are not the only consideration since attention also has to be given to the severity of situations and to the quality of life. This means more than simply applying an agency's eligibility policy and suggests that policies must also be flexible enough to recognise the uniqueness of situations. When coping strategies lack flexibility the uniqueness of individuals and individual need can get lost in the generality of eligibility and depersonalising policies that fail to address service users as individuals but as defined categories which may or may not meet organisationally determined categories of need. Furthermore, social workers may well doubt that agency procedures reflect their experience of services user need or that available resources are most effectively focused, despite policies of prioritisation. We referred earlier to the risk of 'accelerated deterioration' when assessed need remains unmet. It is important also to be clear about what we mean by the phrase 'unmet need' because it has at least two meanings. The first refers to all those needs which might be met but which are not, whilst the second refers to those needs that organisations have a legal duty to meet, or have promised in their policy statements, but have not (Henderson and Atkinson, 2003). The task of recording unmet need is an essential activity of good social work and management practice. Firstly, because responsibility for shortfalls in available resources rests ultimately, in the case of local authorities, with elected members not with social workers or managers. Secondly, failure to quantify and report unmet need makes future service planning more difficult.

What then are the needs and expectations of social workers? Social workers and managers alike have a variety of changing and often conflicting needs and expectations, but the value base of professional practice and decision-making is surely what we share in common. One of the many dangers associated with fears that professional practice is under threat is that social workers believe that their role has now become one of uncritical rationing of resources and administrative practice. This can be seen as a form of 'powerlessness' in which the social worker abandons belief in their ability to contribute positively to alternative approaches:

> *Our senior practitioner recently went to a clinic held by a senior manager. She stressed the team's concerns about needs-led and resource-led assessments and was told that we do not do resource led assessments, even when presented with the evidence that we do.*
>
> (Qualified social worker, 2006)

Summary

This chapter has examined meanings of 'policy' and considered how legal imperatives relate to practice. The influence of policy on practice has been considered from the perspective of the individual, team and organisation. We have specifically regarded policy as a coping mechanism within an environment of change. The tensions between policy and practice, with particular reference to social work values, clearly impacts on delivery and professional morale.

CHAPTER 5

Identity and Culture

> **Key themes in this chapter include:**
> Culture
> Culture and structure
> Identity – personal, professional, organisational
> Accountability
> Blame

Introduction

Upon reflection, it is our perception that every organisation is different and every team within that organisation is in some way different from the next. The 'feel' of teams is different, perhaps their priorities are different, the way they go about their business is different and certainly the personalities that make up those teams are different – even though the overarching aims, objectives and purpose of those teams are fundamentally the same.

But, why are those teams different? What is so unique about them and, most importantly, should they be different? What are the strengths and weaknesses of different teams and, if we find the 'right' way of doing something that works, can we transport those 'hidden' qualities somewhere else in order to create better outcomes in different or failing teams so as to ensure that all service users receive a good and equitable service wherever they are?

In an attempt to answer these questions, it is necessary to consider the concepts of *organisational structure* and *organisational culture* as a way of glimpsing inside organisations and the teams or divisions which make up the organisation. Within this analysis we will consider how much relates to culture and how much relates to structure and how much one relies on the other. We will see if, indeed, culture or structure have any bearing on the success of teams and we will also consider the role of the manager within the social care sector as an important catalyst of change within the culture of the wider organisation or team:

- What is your influence?
- What can you change?

Culture or structure?

Organisational culture is intangible, that is, it is hard to see by those who work in teams or organisations because it represents the norm for those who work within it. Organisational structure, on the other hand, is much more tangible. Structure represents how things are ordered and is more explicit. You may have within your organisation an organisational chart showing where people are within a hierarchy or a flow chart or procedure folder that tells you clearly how the system works and how all the 'parts' fit together to make up the whole. You may have an eligibility or priority criteria schedule which gives some boundaries around what your work actually is, which aids how you structure it. These examples form part of the structure and can, and should, be seen by anyone who joins the team or organisation. Structure involves systems which form part of the processes of the organisation. They can be learnt over time and should be logical and clear and unambiguous. Systems are important and, if not in place, can have dire consequences. Consider Recommendation 19 of Lord Laming's Report into the death of Victoria Climbié:

> *Managers of duty teams must devise and operate a system which enables them immediately to establish how many children have been referred to their team, what action is required to be taken for each child, who is responsible for taking that action, and when that action must be completed.*
>
> (2003: para. 4.14)

If we did not have structure, processes or systems relating to the above, what would the outcome be?

Activity 5.1

Think about your current or recent organisation or team:

- What important structures are currently in place in order to ensure that the needs of service users are being met?
- Can you identify any other areas of your work where you think there should be a structure, process or procedure which doesn't exist?
- If you identified a gap, how easy would it be for you to raise this with your manager and would it be acted upon?

As Rogers (2004: 240) points out, the main focus within recent literature relating to managing structure is concerned with issues such as defining roles, allocating tasks and power differentials. Indeed, we can see from Lord Laming's recommendation that role and task are paramount. Within a multi-professional team setting this might also include processes relating to how knowledge and expertise are shared between team members from different professions. Indeed, the most recent *Working Together to Safeguard Children* document (2006) states that, 'an awareness and appreciation of the role of others is essential for effective collaboration between organisations and their practitioners' (para. 2.1). Can this be achieved through introducing structure or are there other factors that we must consider?

Organisational culture may be part of that structure but over and beyond that it adds to that structure by giving it unconscious meaning in the way that all members of that culture collectively interpret how to carry out their tasks. Handy (1985: 142) notes that:

> *Strong organisations tend to have strong cultures which dominate and permeate the structure and systems. To work in them you have to join them, psychologically as well as physically.*

Organisational culture can be described as a shared cognition or 'mental programme' of 'how we do things around here'.

Schwartz and Davis (1981: 33) argue that culture is:

> *... a pattern of beliefs and expectations shared by the organisation's members that create norms that powerfully shape the behaviour of individuals and groups in the organisation.*

While Hofstede et al. (2005: 4) argue that culture is the collective programming of the mind that distinguishes one group or category of people from others.

Schein (1985: 9) defines organisational culture as:

> *A pattern of basic assumptions invented, discovered or developed by a given group as it learns to cope with its problems of external adaptation and internal integration that has worked well enough to be considered valid and therefore to be taught to new members as the correct way to perceive, think and feel in relation to these problems.*

Activity 5.2

Think about a group that you belong to – the group might be your family, sports group or friendship group.

- Why is your group unique or different from other similar groups?
- There may be outward signs of difference from other groups, for example, dress codes, language used, patterns of interaction, rules etc., but, what actually influences these differences?

Activity 5.3

Think about a time when you started a new job. What was your first day like? As an 'outsider' joining an established team how did you feel? Think about structures within that team. Were they clear and could you define them? Now think about the organisational culture of that team. Could you recognise as an 'outsider' certain things that were going on which were instinctively assumed by others in the team and not by yourself. These may manifest themselves through certain behaviours or attitudes or outlooks or a shared interpretation of meaning. As an 'outsider' you may pick up that something is happening but because you are, at that point, not part of the 'collective consciousness' of that team you may be able to 'see' certain things going on which others who have been in that team or organisation for some time do not see.

List structural elements you have identified within your team or organisation. List as many things as you can that indicated aspects of the organisational culture of the team you were joining. Was it easier to list elements of structure or elements of culture?

Many people, if asked to describe in a sentence the definition of what organisational culture is, might respond 'Well, it's the way we do things around here'. Perhaps it is true to say that you do not even think about it. It is a taken for granted concept which is difficult to define because it is intangible and difficult to measure on its own – although you may measure outcomes or performance indicators or service user feedback or even employee feedback in the form of exit questionnaires. It is only when you join another team that you realise that the culture is different.

Why is understanding organisational culture important?

In the 1980s the idea that the culture of an organisation was important became very prominent. It was felt that if an organisation had a strong organisational culture then everyone knew what their job was and so there was not so great a need to consider strengthening the organisational structure in order for the organisation to be successful. The majority of theorising at this time purely related to the private sector.

From a historical perspective, the rise of interest in organisational culture is likely to be related to socio-economic factors and set within the private organisational realm. Particularly in the 1980s, the western business world wondered why Japanese companies were doing so well as opposed to the US market. Western organisations began to look at Japanese organisations for inspiration. Deal and Kennedy (1982) argued that Japan at that time was one of the more ethically homogeneous nations in the world which placed a great emphasis on conformity within its society. 'The concept of consensus is natural to the Japanese' (Morita, 1987: 198). This conformity was brought into the workplace and formed the organisational culture.

Deal and Kennedy (1982: 5) note:

A major reason the Japanese have been so successful, we think, is their continuing ability to maintain a very strong and cohesive culture throughout the entire country.

However, as we have discussed in previous chapters, current social care departments do not function in a vacuum – they are living organisms and social systems – run by diverse groups of people on behalf of other diverse groups of people and are influenced by the diversity and confusion of what is going on around them. As such, they need permeable boundaries between themselves and the outside world. If there are changes occurring in the external world that need a corresponding change of focus within the organisation, is it possible to implement change as effectively or as quickly as needed if the culture of the organisation is such that it will not allow it? As we will see as we progress through this chapter, it is difficult to change a prevailing culture if it is deeply rooted within 'normal' practice. However, problems arise for the manager if that 'normal practice' is bad practice or dangerous practice or does not fit with external expectations or demands. How does the manager of a social care organisation then change culture and is this always right or necessary or even possible?

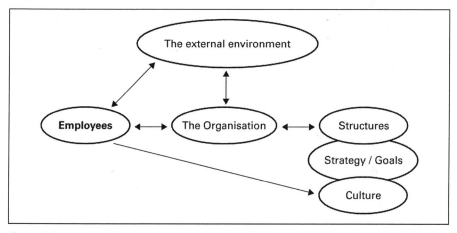

Figure 5.1

As we can see in Figure 5.1, those who work for an organisation are part of the external environment as well as the internal environment of the workplace. The external environment is where they grew up, formed attachments, where they live and where they spend their non-working hours. One might argue that it is the place which predominantly influences them as individuals and a place which nurtures, holds and reinforces their unique identity.

Personal identity

As Hunter clearly states (2003: 323) the role of identity is important in 'marking the relationship between the individual and the social' (Williams and Popay, 1999), whilst Payne (2006: 24) states:

'Identity' in psychology also means the process of seeing ourselves as similar to, modelling ourselves on and valuing another person, for example, being part of a particular family or community. However, feeling the same as some people inevitably involves others being excluded. Therefore, thinking about identity also concerns factors that make us different from others, for example, gender, ethnicity and nationality.

The notion of identity, therefore, derives from where and how people locate themselves within a society or community as well as from the persona that people adopt within prescribed roles within that society or community (Busher, 2005; LaFontaine, 1985; Hollis, 1985).

Adopting this argument, we might further state that as individuals we may simultaneously have several different roles, and therefore identities, at any given time; for example, the role of mother, carer, educator, partner, social worker and the role of manager. The question is, do all our roles form our overall identity?

Activity 5.4

How would you describe your individual identity?

- What are the characteristics which you see as similar to other people and what are the characteristics which make you different from others?
- What aspects of your individual identity do you bring to your professional identity and subsequently influence your role?

Professional identity

Within the workplace individuals also take on a professional identity and subsequently a role identity within the organisation. A professional identity may be seen to be gained from qualification and with that entry into a profession – a social worker, a nurse, a teacher, a police officer. Clearly, entry into the profession means that we accept and 'take on' what that profession stands for – that profession's identity – which may be shaped by many factors.

Professional socialization is the complex process by which a person acquires the knowledge, skills and sense of occupational identity that are characteristic of a member of that profession. It involves the internalization of the values and norms of the group into the person's own behaviour and self conception.

(Jacox, 1973; Cohen, 1981: 14)

Figure 5.2 outlines some of the things that may influence and shape your professional identity.

Payne (2006: 29) usefully offers the following analysis of the professional identity of social care:

- *It is associated with a range of social or welfare services, now called 'social care' in UK official terminology, and in particular healthcare and mental health issues.*

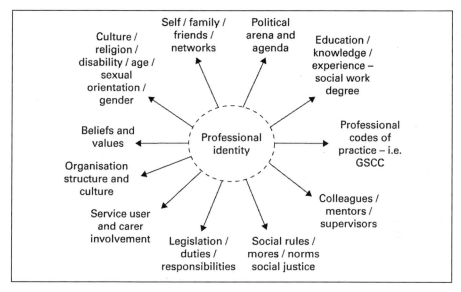

Figure 5.2

- *The services are for people defined as 'deprived' or 'in need' and in particular categories; they are not universal.*
- *Social work involves problem solving for individuals by including counselling and similar activities and through liaison and coordination with official agencies.*
- *It concerns individual human rights, protection and safety for people.*
- *In some understandings, it also involves social change and human empowerment.*

Professional identify also incorporates standards of professional conduct and practice required of social care workers (GSCC – *Codes of Practice for Social Care Workers and Codes of Practice for Employers of Social Care Workers*, September 2002):

Make sure people are suitable to enter the workforce and understand their roles and responsibilities.

(ibid: 4)

As noted by Callero, (1985: 205) 'role identities, by definition, imply action . . . A role can be defined as a set of expectations as to what constitutes role-appropriate behaviour'. Indeed, Terry et al. (1999: 226) argue that the link between self-identity and behavioural intention is predicated on the basis of identity theory which conceives of the self not as a distinct psychological entity, but as a social construct. Terry continues:

Central to identity theory is the view that to understand action – or in more psychological terms, to understand and predict behaviour – it is necessary to conceive of the self and the wider social structure as being inextricably linked. As well as being influenced by the wider social structure, the self is conceived as 'an active creator of social behaviour'.

As such, identity is seen as arising from action and interaction. Indeed, it can be argued that people develop and redefine their professional identity from both the tangible and intangible. Tangible factors may include, for example, position in hierarchy or specific tasks that go with the role whilst intangible factors might include how they are treated and valued by others. The interactions with others act as a continual reinforcement of professional identity. We will expand and offer some thoughts on a 'new' professional identity in Chapter 8.

Identity and the multi-professional team

As we have discussed in previous chapters, the days of the 'single profession' team have made way for an all encompassing model of multi-professional and inter-agency working based on the notions of collaboration, consultation, communication and cohesion. Clear government directives have laid the foundations of how this will look – the rationale is clearly documented, the structure has been mapped and the process has been outlined. But, what about culture? We can easily get people together, we can build our multi-professional team, we can write the procedures, we can even share budgets, but can we break down the barriers of professional identity and culture?

Adams et al. (2006: 55) undertook an investigation into the level of professional identity of students when they commenced their professional studies; the difference in level of professional identity between students from a range of professions; and the factors which might affect the initial levels of professional identification. They concluded that the variables found to be significant predictors of baseline identity were: gender; profession; previous work experience in health and social care environments; understanding of team working; knowledge of profession; and cognitive flexibility. These conclusions reinforce the research of Molyneux (2001) that we discussed in Chapter 3.

Organisational identity

The organisation also has its own identity – Figure 5.3 outlines this in the form of a horizontal flow chart. However, the reality is that these are simultaneous roles that build like layers around the individual as identified in Figure 5.4. As we can see, the layers have permeable boundaries between them and a flow between the layers is identified.

The social care manager, therefore, has to deal with many identities that make up the whole:

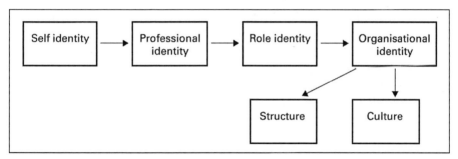

Figure 5.3

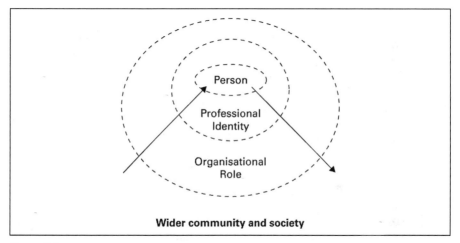

Figure 5.4

- Own individual and professional identity.
- Individual and professional identities of several different professionals who collectively make up the multi-professional team.
- Organisational identity.
- Identity of various and numerous other internal and external stakeholders.
- Identity of community.

It is not surprising, therefore, that difficulties do arise. Lupton (1971) as cited in Buchanan and Huczynski (1985: 330) offers us the useful notion of 'role expectation' to explain how individuals within organisations act:

> *He sometimes does not know how to explain why he behaves the way he does. It's just the 'way we do things here'. In short, people cast other people in roles which are defined by their own expectations. These may be highly*

formal, as legal prescriptions and bureaucratic rules, or they might be informal and implicit, as in custom.

Work colleagues, as social beings, expect regularity and predictability and, as such, expect other colleagues to behave in predictable ways. Change, as we have seen, distorts the equilibrium and creates confusion and unfamiliarity. If not managed well, feelings of conflict may arise whilst others try to regain the equilibrium.

Activity 5.5

You, as an experienced manager of a social care team, have been asked to mentor a less experienced colleague who manages a similar team within the organisation. It appears that your colleague's team is finding it difficult to adapt to new changes in working procedures which have become necessary due to the implementation of different assessment targets. Staff within that team say they are confused about the new procedures and feel less effective in meeting the needs of service users. Some staff within the team have taken more days off sick than usual and the general morale is low.

- How would you try to regain the equilibrium of the team?
- What structural process would you consider implementing in order to effectively manage the necessary change?
- How would you do this within your role as mentor?

Organisational culture

The Social Care Institute of Excellence report, *Developing Social Care: the Current Position* (2005) describes research undertaken by Peck et al. (2002). They looked at the influence of culture in relation to a local service which covered service professionals, other workers and employees and service users in Somerset. As the SCIE report highlights (p.17) the cultural process could be approached in terms of three functions:

- *Culture as a tool of integration, the normative glue holding together diverse actors.*
- *Culture as a tool for understanding the working and difference, the view that overall culture is less significant than complex interaction between multiple sub-cultures, such as professional affiliations.*
- *Culture as a tool of individuals, stressing that 'culture is an enactment neither [solely] of management manipulation nor of professional subculture, but rather the ebb and flow of individual relationships'.*

Perhaps one useful way of expanding on the above is by looking at culture with the assistance of the 'Cultural Web' which is outlined by Johnson and Scholes (1999: 75).

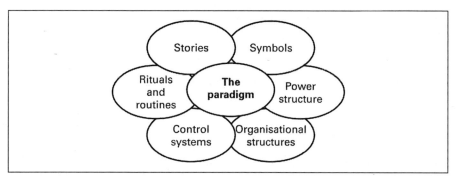

Figure 5.5

The Cultural Web is a representation of the taken-for-granted assumptions of an organisation and the physical manifestations of organisational culture. It is necessary to briefly expand on these elements:

Routine: the way that individuals within the organisation or team relate to one another and towards those who are not part of the team. As Johnson and Scholes point out (ibid.) it can form the 'taken-for-granted' about how things should happen and this can be extremely difficult to change.

Rituals: of organisational life are the special events through which the organisation emphasises what is important. Rituals can take on both a formal and an informal nature. For example, the after work socialisation of the team on a Friday evening.

Symbols: are perhaps more easy to see; the organisation logo, the terminology or language adopted which have evolved over time and only those who work within that team, or even profession, know what they mean. For example, all child care social workers will understand what is meant by LAC (*looked after child*) or CAF (*common assessment framework*) or SAP (*single assessment process*). Clearly, nurses, teachers and police officers have their own terminology. Adams et al. (2002: 10) outline the importance of language and our constructed understanding of the world. Increasingly, as multi-professional teams are formed, the language of professions will change to accommodate shared meaning and understanding and form part of a shared culture.

Stories: grow up over time within the team or organisation and become a form of reinforcing and restating the bonding of those who know or were involved with the incident or action from where the story arose. Perhaps they arise from a team away day or past changes that have happened within the organisation or team or the past restructuring. Social workers who have worked within the profession for many years, for example, might recall what it was like doing social work in the 1980s with some positive reflection. Stories told in this way can, therefore, reinforce to newcomers, some form of hierarchy based on experience.

Power: can also be seen as formal and informal. Perhaps you know of teams where actually the most powerful person does not have the most senior position but rather power is contained within the function that that person performs. It may be a myth or reality but it is certainly an assumption that the doctor's receptionist holds the most power when patients are trying to gain an appointment. Power is of crucial importance within the culture of organisations, particularly in relation to professional roles within a multi-professional team. As social workers we may have an idea about our profession being more powerful than other service sector professions, but, similarly, other professional groups may have similar ideas about their profession. It is the manager's role to quickly ensure equity and reduce role ambiguity or role confusion at such times as, invariably, the service user can 'get lost' within this type of debate.

Control systems: emphasise how and what is valued within an organisation. Are we controlled by the quality of service that we provide for a service user or are we controlled by performance indicators? As social workers we are caught up within the debate of 'who are we here for', 'who controls what we do' and 'who determines our focus'. Perhaps, in this latest epoch of social work some might say that we are controlled by paperwork or bureaucracy whilst others maintain a casework or therapeutic lead to what they do. We have previously argued that another form of control is our 'professional code of practice'. Within a multi-professional team the added dimension or dilemma is that currently professionals have their own forms of control. What takes precedence? Is there a hierarchy? How can the skilful and experienced manager weave or blend these together?

Johnson and Scholes (ibid.) argue that the combination of all of these elements determines the 'paradigm' of the organisational culture, while Nohria and Eccles (1992) argue that the choice of rhetoric and strategic action is conditioned by the past actions and experiences of an organisation.

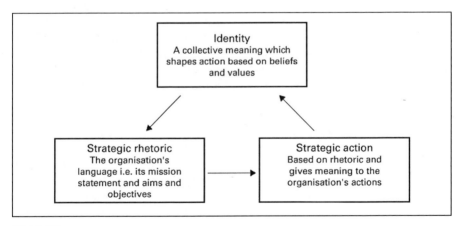

Figure 5.6

In an informative article, Higgins et al. (2004: 63) argue that to successfully manage organisational culture, managers must manage 'cultural artefacts' which they describe as:

Myths and sagas about company successes and the heroes and heroines within the company; language systems and metaphors; rituals, ceremonies, and symbols; certain physical attributes such as the use of space, interior and exterior design and equipment; and the defining values and norms.

Activity 5.6

Think of a team or organisation that you have worked in and the elements represented in the Cultural Web. Write down at least one example of these elements that you have observed. What elements were easy to interpret and what elements were more difficult and less tangible? How useful have you found undertaking this activity as a way of gaining insight into your organisation? Has it made you think more deeply about things that you may have previously taken for granted? How important are these things for your team or organisation? How easy would it be to change them? Are they always positive and do they add to the effectiveness of the team or task?

Stories _____

Symbols _____

Power _____

Rituals and Routines _____

Controls _____

Structure _____

Activity 5.7

Referring back to the scenario presented in Activity 5.3, what cultural aspects of the team might you consider to be barriers that step in the way of the proposed change. How useful is the cultural web in formulating your ideas about what is going on in this team?

When considering change it is important to have an overall view of the components which make up the whole. The McKinsey 7-S framework (Have et al., 2003) defines seven elements of an organisation and suggests that only when all seven elements are in harmony, supporting and being supported by each other, can the organisation be considered to be 'organised'.

As we can see from Figure 5.7, shared values are at the centre of the culture of the organisation or team and all other elements that make up the whole are influenced by culture. Similarly, there is a mutuality in that culture itself is influenced by those elements.

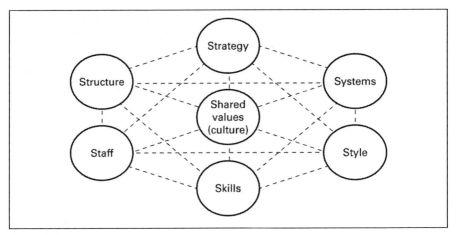

Figure 5.7

Accountability and blame

As we have noted, individual, professional and organisational identity is acquired by certain characteristics that make up the whole. In a professional sphere we considered the synergy between professional identity and professional role. Role, however, brings with it responsibilities and levels of accountability.

We can highlight two main ways in which accountability operates within the social care sector:

- professional accountability: day to day contact with colleagues which may be on a casual basis or more formally in team meetings.
- managerial accountability: contact with anyone who you are responsible to for your work which is usually expressed in the form of 'supervision'.

It can be argued that supervision is an example of the way in which some teams and organisations formalise the structure of accountability. Lishman (1994) however, disagrees with the managerial definition of supervision and sees it as something different from management control and accountability because it is built on a 'professional to professional relationship rather than superior to subordinate one' (ibid: 39). We will expand on the role of supervision in future chapters.

Consider the scenario below:

Activity 5.8

You are a newly qualified social worker who has been visiting a family for several months. The pre-school age children are placed on the child protection register due to concerns about neglect. The parents have asked you to visit today as someone from the benefits agency is attending and they feel they want your support. It has taken several weeks of difficult visits with this family to get to a point where they willingly agree to you seeing the children. When you arrive the person from the benefits agency is already there and you walk into the sitting room and join the gathering. You cannot believe your eyes – where once stood the nice three piece suite, now there is a couple of old chairs, where once the floor was laid with good carpet, now there are floor boards. The family begin to tell the benefits officer that they need money so that their young children can walk on the floor without getting wood splinters in their feet. You are speechless and have not encountered this sort of behaviour before. You make your excuses to leave and return to speak to your manager about what you should do. When you confront the family later, they advise you that the furniture and carpet is 'stored' in the garden shed and, 'not to worry as it will be back in the home that evening'.

- Should you inform the benefits agency?
- You are the manager of this social worker – what would you advise and why?
- To what stakeholder does your accountability lie?

To many of us it seems that we live and work in a world of blame. The train fails to run on time and this is blamed on wet leaves on the track; the delivery we were waiting for does not arrive and the organisation blames it on the delivery person not picking the item up at the warehouse. The list is never ending.

Clearly, within the teams and organisations where we work, we also hear talk of a blame culture. When something goes wrong someone has to be accountable and therefore someone has to be blamed. 'Accountable' seems like a positive notion whilst blame always appears negative.

Activity 5.9
You are a manager of a privately-run residential home. An elderly resident falls over whilst walking to the day room. Thankfully, the elderly person does not sustain any physical injuries but is, nevertheless, quite distressed. The care assistant who is accountable for the care of this resident is beside herself and is blaming herself for not being with her at all times.

- As a manager how would you deal with this situation?
- Who are the main stakeholders you are accountable to?
- How would you deal with the blame that the care worker has expressed?

Summary
This chapter began by introducing the concept of identity. We highlighted identity relating to the individual, profession, role and organisation. We have

noted that organisations are made up of elements which are sometimes considered to be 'hard' – strategy, structure, systems – and 'soft' – staff, skills, style. Central to all of these is the concept of shared values or culture. We have explored some key thoughts as to how culture may be 'seen' within an organisation. When talking about change and managing change it is important to consider not only the structure that has to change, but, more importantly, that culture also has to change – a cultural shift has to take place. It may be relatively easy to change the blocks of structure because they are easy to see and can be manipulated to 'fit' with what is needed. Changing structure to create change is sometimes seen as the quick option but on its own can never be entirely successful. Culture, however, is less tangible and embedded within a team or organisation and enacted in different ways that are difficult to unpick and reassemble. Culture is important as it can stand in the way of change and can promote hidden barriers that people put up to stop change happening. Further, we may not wish to change everything as some aspects of an organisation's culture can be positive.

The present day social care manager works with complexity and change within complexity and change. Equilibrium is something that social care workers strive for when dealing with societal difficulties and those within society who need support and stability. It is ironical that social care workers try to create that stability for others but sometimes it seems that this is never afforded to themselves within the organisation. Social care workers as individuals and as part of a team or organisation look to the manager to create some kind of order that they can hold onto during times of change.

CHAPTER 6

Managing Performance

> **Key themes in this chapter include:**
> Driving forces
> Value for money
> Performance management
> Quality and standards
> Reflection

Introduction: driving forces

A significant influence on social work practice and on the public sector generally is the introduction of methods and approaches more familiar to business than to social care. At the heart of this change has been the arrival of performance management as an integral part of modern governance. Before discussing the characteristics of performance management, it is helpful to first consider the wider context of political and practice influences.

As we discussed earlier, the Labour government, elected in 1997, while expressing a determination to improve the quality of public services, was equally keen to show that it was committed to obtain the best value for the taxpayer. Along with the drive for greater accountability, however, is the taxpayers' right to know how their money is being spent and that services are being provided efficiently and effectively.

To a large extent the Labour government continued the reform of public services introduced by the Conservative government first elected in 1979. They were highly critical of the monopoly provision of social services through local authorities which they regarded as inefficient, bureaucratic and unresponsive to the needs of service users. They were concerned too by the escalating costs of welfare provision and the economic recession of the 1970s and 1980s gave rise to serious doubt that the welfare state was any longer affordable. The idea that the state has a responsibility to meet all welfare needs was superseded by the idea that the state's responsibility was to enable informal carers or the community to provide care. Since that time we have seen a movement away from the one-to-one focus of traditional social work practice towards the encouragement of self- help by individuals, family networks and communities. Social services departments have become assessors of need and purchasers of services rather than providers. It is in this context that performance management becomes a central activity for change aimed at securing greater efficiency and effectiveness in the delivery and management of services. This focus, however, demands additional skills and approaches to those traditionally associated with social work practice.

It is helpful to see the current emphasis on performance through a comparison with practice in the 1960s and 1970s where social services were administered as a professional bureaucracy that, reflecting expertise, allowed social workers a high degree of discretion (Adams, 1998: 57). Documentation was needed when exercising statutory powers or complying with regulations for children in public care but there were few standardised forms for monitoring and practitioners had considerable autonomy (Munro, 2004). In a study of social services departments in the 1970s Parsloe and Stevenson drew attention to the 'wide ranging freedom which social workers had to choose the style and content of their direct work with clients' (1978: 134). One significant feature of practice was the importance placed on the relationship between social worker and client as an essential means for achieving 'change' (Hollis, 1992). Skills of empathy and intuition were highly valued and these were considered to lie beyond 'objective' study by the positivist research methods that were dominant at the time (Munro, 2004).

Although the complexities of psycho-social casework, based on Freudian theory, attracted its critics it did provide a theoretical base to practice albeit mainly for the specialists in psychiatric and child care social work. It was not, however, conducive to meeting emerging demands for greater transparency and accountability with defined aims and time-limited agreements between client and social worker. It was difficult to reach a conclusion about the effectiveness of social work intervention without detailed knowledge of what had been done so that this could inform future practice.

It was not practice methods alone that were being questioned, as concerns were also being voiced about the cost of services. Until the mid 1990s, there was a general failure on the part of local authorities to link costs of services to performance. Few authorities could detail how many people received services, at what standard and at what cost. Nor did they know whether assessments were carried out promptly or if services delivered the outcomes that service users required. The phenomenon of clients 'drifting' within 'the system' for years was commonplace.

Misgivings about the purpose, value and effectiveness of social work led to a realisation, not least within the profession itself, that action needed to be taken to articulate social work practice more clearly. In particular that practice should become more transparent and accountable to the community.

- **Sets objectives:** What you want to achieve expressed in terms of short, medium and long term goals.
- **Inputs:** Resources you use to produce a service or execute a policy expressed in terms of finance, human resources, equipment and needs of users.
- **Outputs:** What you actually achieve. Services produced expressed in terms of quantity and quality.
- **Sets targets:** What you want to achieve broken down into manageable parts.
- **Performance indicators:** The evidence used to judge how well a person or organisation has performed.
- **Monitoring:** Collecting information to judge performance.
- **Reflection:** Looking back on your experience. What you did well or may want to do differently in future.

Figure 6.1

Key features of performance management

Effective organisations need to have clearly defined objectives and outcomes and, in order to secure them, explicit targets need to be set. It follows that there must be performance measures or indicators of the progress achieved, and performance monitoring to determine success or failure (Henderson and Atkinson, 2003). The key features of performance management can be summarised in the following way:

Managers and social workers are increasingly subject to levels of external scrutiny that are unknown in commercial organisations. Social care managers are accountable to politicians and other tiers of government and to independent inspectorates. The rationale for performance management is that accountability is strengthened because the public is able to see how service providers are performing.

(Baggini, 2000)

It provides a means of enabling social care organisations to demonstrate their ability to deliver on a range of different service objectives. Underpinning this approach is the belief that, by reorganising the delivery of services and applying appropriate management techniques, resources can be employed more efficiently and effectively. That is to say at a lower cost, getting the greatest benefit from resources available.

Activity 6.1

Using the key features identified in Figure 6.1, outline how performance management impacts on the quality of service to service users. Use a SWOT analysis as a way of framing your response.

Value for money

It is interesting at this point to note how thinking about cost has developed. Under the Conservative government of 1979, the introduction of compulsory competitive tendering implied going for the cheapest option, whereas under New Labour this was replaced by a move towards 'Best Value' which can be seen as the achievement of the most advantageous combination of cost and quality (Coulshed and Mullender, 2006).

Best Value was introduced by the government in April 2000 with the impetus of increasing the emphasis on quality and improving services. It required local authorities to review the services they provide using the 'four Cs';

- *Challenging* why and how the service is provided.
- *Comparing* performance with others, including independent and voluntary sector providers.
- *Competing* by using fair and open competition.
- *Consulting* service users and residents on their expectations of services.

Figure 6.2

The concept of value for money is central to performance and has justified a wide range of reviews and re-organisations, cost reduction programmes and approaches to cutting waste. It requires the commissioning and delivery of services to be based not just on economy and efficiency, but also on effectiveness and quality:

- **Economy:** is about the cost of inputs used – quality at the lowest cost.
- **Efficiency:** is the relationship between inputs (resources used) and outputs (services produced). Greater efficiency is achieved by increasing outputs or reducing inputs, for example, cost reduction.
- **Effectiveness:** is the extent to which policy objectives are achieved and are, therefore, concerned with outcomes.

It is important to note that effectiveness is significantly different from the first two since it more directly relates to outcomes and thus to the service user experience. 'Benefits' (as outcomes) can be very difficult to measure. How, for example, can social and psychological benefits to service users be measured? Such benefits are notional and depend on the individual perception of the service recipient. They cannot be priced in real financial terms and, consequently, measures of efficiency rely heavily on outputs that are usually measured in terms of quantity. What actually happens as a result of providing a service is arguably a more reliable insight to quality.

Value for money remains an important objective but 'Best Value' provides a framework for continuous service improvement and places a stronger emphasis on change by encouraging managers to think how best they can deliver their services (Lapsley and Pong, 2000: 546).

Operational tensions

Social workers and managers in the public sector often feel they are being pulled in different directions. Faced with budgetary pressures and conflicting demands from different stakeholders it is particularly difficult in social care to determine priorities and set a coherent agenda for change. The relationship with politicians, who set the framework in which organisations operate is critical but, as we observed in Chapter 3, social and political expectations, along with the complex nature of service demands present a unique set of challenges.

For social workers there are mounting tensions between organisational policies to improve financial management and the demands of professional practice in which social workers see themselves as primarily caring people concerned with human rather than fiscal policy. It would not be surprising if practitioners felt pulled in several directions overwhelmed by 'urgent' priorities, frustrated with the pace of change and under constant pressure to deliver both agendas and meet the demands of local services.

Performance management, Mullins (2002) suggests, is intended to increase managerial control to ensure greater efficiency and effectiveness but this becomes counter-productive in instances where control becomes an end in itself. It is in this context that criticism of the Performance Assessment Framework can best be understood.

Performance Assessment Framework

The Performance Assessment Framework for social services in England was announced in the White Paper, *Modernising Social Services* (DoH, 1998). This was a major initiative which had a significant impact on the management and organisation of services and on social work practice. It identified a range of indicators for all social services, to be collected in each local authority and collated nationally as the basis for publishing comparative data on performance.

Most social workers have heard of performance indicators but many may not be clear what they are. At a political level indicators have become important because they are used by the government as a major source of evidence about a social services department's performance (Munroe, 2004). They identify key areas where information about the service performance of an organisation should be gathered. They also identify a level of performance that the organisation should meet. Typically, they measure such things as response times, referral rates, service waiting times and the like. These can be evaluated against costs, resources and staffing levels. Gathering and collating information in this way enables comparisons to be made between local authorities and, as such, serve as a quality monitoring tool. Importantly, they are the measures by which the service is held accountable.

The system is based around five performance domains which are the same as those used for the Best Value Performance Indicators established for most local government services. These are:

- *National priorities and objectives* – the extent to which councils with social services responsibilities are delivering national and local strategic objectives.
- *Cost and efficiency* – provide cost effective services.
- *Effectiveness of service delivery and outcomes* – delivering services appropriate to need, in line with best practice; to agreed standards; timely; appropriately trained staff; using resources to increase self-sufficiency, social and economic participation; to increase life chances of looked after children; provide safe and supportive services.
- *Quality of services for users and cares* – involvement in assessment and review; experiences of service; responsiveness; continuity of provision.
- *Fair access* – fairness of provision in relation to need; access in relation to need; clear eligibility criteria; accessible information about provision.

Critical reflection

The introduction of performance indicators was initially criticised because insufficient attention was given to quality and although these have in the main been addressed, there remain a number of conceptual and practical problems.

First, when the government talks about wanting to improve a service, it does so without knowing what improvement may mean in a given context. Critics have argued that social workers are better placed to decide what represents improvement and what actually needs to be spent. That will, of course, always be a matter for negotiation, since it depends also on how much is available. Second, there are dangers as well as advantages in seeking to 'measure' social work. It has on the one hand the advantage of providing a clear criterion by which to judge success. There is a risk, however, that performance indicators become a straightjacket that detracts from responding flexibly to the unique and infinitely varied needs of service users. The third difficulty relates to resource availability, since this will always influence outcomes. A favourable outcome for children services, for example, may be fewer children accommodated, but if there are no alternatives to accommodation because preventative services are insufficient or unavailable, this outcome is unlikely to be met.

> Activity 6.2
> You are a team manager in a team that supports adolescents in need.
> You have very clear messages from your senior managers that unless
> there is significant risk, adolescents should not be accommodated

(S.20 Children Act 1989). One of your experienced social workers has approached you as, although their assessment has indicated that there is not significant risk, the young adolescent's main and only carer has refused to take him back home and he is now homeless and sitting in the reception area with a small bag of belongings. The senior social worker believes that accommodation should be sought for this young person.

- What actions and decision would you take as the manager of the team as to whether the young person should be accommodated?
- How would you justify the decision that you make to both the social worker and the senior manager?
- Would your actions and decision be any different if you looked at the situation from the perspective of your professional social work identity?

The results of joint reviews and performance outcomes are often used in the construction of league tables showing the rank order of local authorities. League tables may serve to strengthen accountability because the public is able to see how services are performing. The emphasis on efficiency and effectiveness is also re-inforced via publicly-available inspection reports (Baggini, 2000), but these advantages also have to be balanced by the negative consequences for staff morale and motivation, because league tables are unable to accurately reflect particular circumstances such as:

- Availability of resources.
- Quality of work produced by the social worker.
- Interpersonal skills of staff.
- Commitment to finding alternatives for service users.

There is perhaps a certain inevitability that in a climate of competing pressures and priorities it can be easier to blame the pressures on the government's agenda. For some it remains a struggle to reconcile a conflict between the 'legitimate' power of government and the 'expert' power of professionals (French and Raven, 1959) in determining what is good practice. As an ex-student recently commented:

I see targets and statistics as something that I produce for 'higher manage-ment' not as something for myself because it informs my practice.

The student's comments illustrate the conceptual and practical difficulties of performance management, but we must not allow these to overshadow the part that objectives, targets and outcomes play in effective social work practice. The social work assessment, for example, has all the key features of performance management.

Activity 6.3
Using a Force Field analysis as outlined in Figure 1.1 outline the conflicts and dilemmas that you face between, on the one hand, performance management indicators and on the other social work practice realities.

- As a social care manager how do you implement and embed a culture of performance management within your team or organisation?
- What resistance might you encounter and how do you deal with this?

Despite the shortcomings discussed it is important to recognise that social workers do have the autonomy to exercise professional judgement in the best interest of service users. Often they have considerable discretion in the use of resources by deciding, for example, what level of service to provide. Sometimes it may feel as if the objectives of the organisation are in conflict with professional values as we discussed previously. To believe that the solution is simply a matter of additional resources is to ignore the realities of supply and demand and the finite nature of resources. In our personal lives, we know that, if we continue to spend more of our personal income than we receive each month, the ultimate consequence is bankruptcy, and so it is for social care organisations.

Social workers and managers work in a world of complexity, uncertainty and ambiguity (Southon and Braithwaite, 1998). Performance management with its commitment to targets, performance measures, scrutiny, appraisal and monitoring, represents a clear challenge to all those engaged in social care. Part of this challenge is how social work responds to changing demands and expectations as we become increasingly more accountable to taxpayers and service users. Another is learning to become more responsible for our own practice, more creative, better problem-solvers, and less reliant on 'yesterday's solutions'. We will return to this challenge later in the chapter but first consider the concept of quality.

What is quality?

The word 'quality' has suffered over the years by being used to describe attributes such as expensiveness and above all, luxury. We might, for example, describe a car as a 'quality car' when, in reality, it is an expensive or luxurious car. Cloth might be described as a 'quality cloth' when it is 'all wool', or a cloth that has a high density of threads (Munroe-Faure and Munroe-Faure, 1992). If the concept of quality is hard to define in the commercial world it is even more difficult in interpersonal professions such as social work.

Quality implies excellence or at least the pursuit of excellence but what does this mean in practice? Coulshed and Mullender (2006: 57) believe that quality means providing services that are fit for purpose, but doing so at a reasonable cost with due regard for ensuring informed choice on the part of those using them. This implies that the ultimate test of quality will always be what users and their families think of the services we provide. *A Quality Strategy for Social Care* (DoH, 2000) describes quality as a process of changing and improving services, that:

- Meet high standards.
- Are responsive and appropriate.
- Enable participation in society.
- Involve users so choice is informed.

Quality is not informed by service users alone. In addition the public, elected members of local authorities, boards of trustees, management committees and central government all have an interest in matters of quality. While hard to define it is possible to determine what it means in practice since service users will know the experience of a good service that is 'fit for purpose' as they can also recognise the experience of a poor one. Thus first hand experience according to some commentators is what determines quality.

Measuring quality

The introduction of quality control through inspection involves monitoring services against performance standards which, as we observed earlier in the chapter, means using statistical and other systematically gathered information to check that services are meeting agreed standards. Quality control, dominated by standards and performance indicators, pays insufficient attention, critics argue, to factors such as resource availability that can also influence performance. Neither is the approach able to identify the extent to which practice has exceeded standards, only whether or not they have been met or reached (Henderson and Atkinson, 2003).

Measuring the quantitative elements of service is relatively easy to do, but as James (1992: 51) points out:

The problem is that many of the same mechanisms are used to promote quality as to effect management control (information systems, policy and procedural guides, review, inspection and appraisal). It is all too easy therefore, for a manager to talk quality but mean control and for staff to hear quality but understand it as control.

Just as quality is difficult to define it is also a difficult concept to promote, particularly amongst those who regard quality control processes as a proliferation of bureaucracy that is expensive and time-consuming; money that might otherwise be channelled into providing direct services.

Approaches to quality

Approaches to quality have to be seen within their historical context and, as we have argued previously, it was against the background of initiatives by central government that quality became an increasingly high profile activity in social care in the 1980s. First, there was concern about poor practice and performance in social care which prompted both Conservative (1979) and Labour (1997) governments to initiate agendas for change that introduced, among other things, competition – in the belief that this would improve quality. Second, financial pressures meant that it was no longer possible to improve quality by increasing levels of expenditure and services. As a consequence, the emphasis on quality shifted to improvement through greater efficiency and cost effectiveness with the introduction of a new management culture. A third influence was the growth of pressure groups which challenged the notion of professional autonomy and argued for greater user involvement in service design, delivery and evaluation.

Professional concerns were less to do with the concept of quality, but rather that the model introduced was essentially a commercial model. It is often argued that social care is unsuited to such an approach, because of the nature of services, which are not concerned to increase organisational profit. There is, on the other hand, much to commend the pursuit of a more business-like, effective and cost efficient service, although these objectives become discredited if in practice they mean service reductions to manage other organisational pressures.

As our ex-student remarked earlier, the top-down, reactive nature of quality control is often perceived by practitioners as a negative experience, whereas quality assurance is more proactive in that it involves putting measures into place and, as such, has a preventative purpose. It is also a more 'grass-roots' approach that tends to involve staff more in the process of delivering better services to people (Coulshed and Mullender, 2006).

Most social work services need to ask subjective and process-related questions such as the extent to which users feel in control of their lives and able to influence services they receive and are treated as a person by staff (Qureshi, 1998). It is important, however, to recognise that quality assurance is not just about assessment of quality, but includes the mechanism to support and promote quality through, for example, procedures, policies, training, appraisal and service delivery. It also, importantly, relates to the supervision process which we will explore further in Chapter 7.

Quality control and quality assurance are both essential activities to promote best possible services. In the past, professional approaches to quality were concerned with inputs and process rather than outcomes. Typically, a professional approach is assessed through skills and competence in practice with quality embedded in the core values. The weakness of this approach, as

Henderson and Atkinson (2003) point out, is that it is essentially an introspective process within the profession which excludes the service user. So what conclusion can we reach about quality? Quality above all means improving services to those who use them and it is the quality of the user's experience that matters. In this, responsibility for quality rests with each and every member of staff and volunteer and is the first responsibility of every manager (Warr and Kelly,1992: 5).

Influence of standards

Quality social work is informed by standards supported by a sound knowledge base and a wide range of skills and competences. First, though, we need to be conversant with the National Occupational Standards for Social Work.

The General Social Care Council, established under the Care Standards Act 2000, came into being in October 2001 to:

> ... *promote the highest standards of social care in England for the benefit and protection of people who use services and the wider public.*

(GSCC, 2002: 1)

Established to regulate social care staff, including social workers, the GSCC has established a Code of Practice for Social Workers which describes the required standards of professional practice and conduct. There has been much debate about what constitutes an acceptable level of practice.

The National Occupational Standards for Social Work identify six key roles:

- Prepare for, and work with, individuals, families, carers, groups and communities to assess their needs and circumstances.
- Plan, carry out, review and evaluate social work practice, with individuals, families, carers, groups, communities and other professionals.
- Support individuals to represent their needs, views and circumstances and to achieve greater independence.
- Manage risk to individuals, families, carers, groups, communities, self and colleagues.
- Manage to be accountable, with supervision and support, for their own practice within their organisation.
- Demonstrate and be responsible for professional competence in social work practice.

Alongside these six key roles, the Code of Practice for Social Care Workers, which includes social workers, states that workers must:

- Protect the rights and promote the interests of service users and carers.
- Strive to establish and maintain the trust and confidence of users and carers.
- Promote the independence of service users while protecting them as far as possible from danger or harm.

- Respect the rights of service users whilst seeking to ensure that their behaviour does not harm themselves or other people.
- Uphold public trust and confidence in social care services.
- Be accountable for the quality of their work and take responsibility for maintaining and improving their knowledge and skills.

Whilst these two documents provide agreed standards and expectations of practice, the issue of standards is far from straightforward. The Standards of Practice, Munro (2004) suggests, are those which are most likely to lead to the desired outcomes for service users by the most economic, efficient and ethical means. Clearly, standards are needed to interpret evidence of performance that counts as good or bad practice. This is particularly difficult for social work in the absence of valid, reliable measures of key variables of human behaviour. As we suggested earlier, outcomes are influenced by many factors other than professional intervention, for example, external judgements on practice taken at moments in time which provide no indication of long term sustainability. Without a more evaluative study it is not possible to say whether prescribed standards of good practice lead to better outcomes although this is not to suggest that the introduction of national standards is any less important. Indeed, they provide an essential baseline and framework for practice, but standards of good practice rely heavily on professional wisdom and as we have emphasised, most importantly, the experience of service users.

> ### Activity 6.4
> Consider the work of your team or organisation. In what ways do you, or could you, include service user input into standards of good practice?
> - What service user input gaps within existing policies and practice can you identify?
> - How would you narrow those gaps?
> - Formulate an action plan that indicates your gap analysis and what actions you would take. Use the six National Occupational Standards as your framework.

Practice knowledge and skills

The knowledge base of social work is considerable and constantly growing as the profession faces new challenges and approaches to practice, driven by political, technological, social and economic influences. Increasingly, social workers are engaged in planning, organising and controlling resources which have historically been seen exclusively as the province of management. The role has shifted from direct intervention to one calling for knowledge of costs, commissioning, organisational policies, systems and, at an interpersonal level, awareness of factors that influence internal and external organisational behaviour and relationships. New expectations have exposed inadequacies in the knowledge base of social work, social care management and leadership, and have demanded approaches that challenge the value base of practice. It is not surprising that social workers, faced with challenges such as tackling oppression and discrimination in society, should find these 'new expectations' daunting and far removed from traditional categories of knowledge that informs professional practice such as law, human development and the social context of knowledge. Indeed, many of the problems encountered in practice are social in origin as a result of poverty, deprivation and exclusion. Class, race, ethnicity, gender, age, disability, sexual identity and religion are important ways in which people's lives are influenced and constrained by social factors relating to the distribution of opportunities and life chances (Thompson, 2005: 59).

Sound assessment is at the heart of good social work practice. It is through gathering information that the social worker is able to form a picture of individuals in their life situation and, on the basis of this information, identify needs and what services should be provided. This is a somewhat simplistic view of a complex process in which understanding the causation of problems is essential if action plans are to be effective and efficient. In assessment, the social worker draws on knowledge gained from research, theoretical frameworks and concepts that inform understanding of presenting problems or provide a basis for hypothesising causation and as such, it is a task that requires considerable skill and knowledge. Effective assessment practice involves gathering information, setting clear objectives, having a strategy for achieving them and knowing what determines a successful service outcome. It is an on-going process in which progress is reviewed and monitored and, once completed, evaluated in order to learn what went well and what might be done differently in future.

Systematic assessment is fundamental to both good practice and to good management, but it also offers a further dimension to understanding performance management, since the core activities of gathering information, planning, setting objectives, monitoring and reviewing are key features that the two share in common.

Having a sound knowledge base is not enough, and indeed it could be argued that no amount of theoretical understanding can compensate for a lack of the interpersonal skills necessary for effective practice. In 1996 the Central Council for Education and Training in Social Work identified six skills and competences that social work students needed to demonstrate while on placement in order to establish that they were fit to practice:

1. **Communicate and engage:** *competencies involve being able to communicate effectively with significant others including service users, carers, other members of the community and colleagues internal and external to the organisation.*

2. *Promote and engage:* *promote opportunities for people to use their own strengths and expertise to enable them to meet their responsibilities, secure rights and achieve change.*
3. *Assess and plan:* *identified as central to the social work role.*
4. *Intervene and provide services:* *competence to intervene and provide services is closely related to assessment and the action plans drawn up as a result of it. It involves commissioning services and 'managing through others', managing risk, and managing change.*
5. *Work in organisations:* *being part of a team, working effectively with external organisations. Being a responsible and accountable practitioner in the context of organisational policies and procedures.*
6. *Develop professional competence:* *the importance of ongoing professional development to improve competence, knowledge and skills.*

(CCETSW, 1996: 11)

So far we have been concerned with an introduction to knowledge and skills and their relationship to professional practice. We next identify a number of skills that contribute to individual performance and effectiveness.

First we consider social workers as 'problem-solvers'. Problem-solving is an essential function of social work which, together with assessment, decision-making and communication, is a skill we should be seeking to develop.

Problem solving

Much of what social workers and managers do is 'solve problems' and to make decisions, often by reacting to them. We may feel stressed and often short of time and, consequently, when we encounter a new problem or decision to take, we react with a decision that seemed to work before. It is easy with this approach to get stuck in a cycle of solving the same problem over and over again in the same way and it is therefore important to stop, think, and reflect and adopt an organised and systematic approach to problem-solving and decision-making. This is often more complex than is sometimes described, particularly where it involves working in complex situations for which there may be no ideal solution. Not all problems can be solved nor decisions made by a purely rational approach. However, the following basic guidelines can provide a helpful framework:

1. Identify problem

Whenever you detect a problem, try to recognise it as a separate event. All too often we fail to be effective because we do not separate out the problem from other events and from the circumstances that surround it. Being able to recognise the problem requires the ability to understand its nature and this is an important part of the process of assessment.

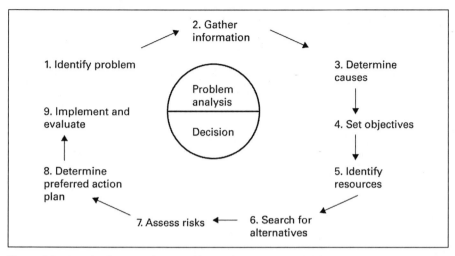

Figure 6.3 Standard approach to problem solving: some guidelines

Write down a clear description of what the problem is. If a problem is not clearly understood, then the likelihood of a chosen solution being successful is unlikely.

Problems are often one of two types. Either they are (1) obstacles, conditions that get in the way of achieving the desired outcome, or, (2) they are obstacles which are causing a deviation from the desired state.

An example of a problem might be that children with a learning disability are often unable to receive respite care because of local authority funding shortfalls. The desired result may be that children should have monthly respite care available to them. The funding shortfall is an obstacle that stands in the way of achieving the desired outcome.

2. Gather information

Collecting information is necessary in the process of analysing the problem and can be drawn from many sources, for example, from specific policy documents such as the *Framework for the Assessment of Children in Need and their Families, Community Care Assessment* or from knowledge, experience, research and so on.

You need to ask:

- What do I need to know?
- How can I gather the necessary information?
- What options does the information give me?

3. Determine causes

Thinking about possible causes is part of the social work assessment process and an important step in problem solving. The previous step, gathering information, may give you some insight into what the causes could be. Start by asking:

- How can I precisely define the problem?
- Exactly when did it occur?
- What changed to cause the problem?
- What assumptions am I making about the causes?
- Are there times when this problem could have occurred, but didn't?
- How urgent/serious is it?

4. Set objectives

Objective setting clarifies as precisely as possible the desired outcome. This provides focus and direction to the problem solving. The outcome of your problem solving should be consistent with professional values. Ask the questions:

- What could I aim towards?
- What should I aim towards?
- What are the important implications of my choice?

5. Identify resources

Never an easy task but start by asking the question, *'What have I got that I can use to solve the problem?'* Your examination ought to cover three basic, critical resources:

1. People resources – who is available to help, and do they have the skills and knowledge?;
2. Financial – what can be spent; limits of financial authority. Could available funding be spent differently?;
3. Physical – where the work can be done. Availability of resources.

6. Search for alternatives

- Use knowledge and experience already available, as ready-made solutions may already exist. Seek ideas from others.
- Ask penetrating questions: What is being done? Who else can do it? Where else can it be done? How might I do it differently?
- Think creatively 'there are no unanswerable questions, there are only people who ask the wrong questions'.

7. Assess risks

The next step is concerned with assessing the advantages and disadvantages of each alternative:

- Identify risks.
- Identify the likely costs.
- Assess strengths and weaknesses and give each weighting on a 1 to 10 scale.

8. Determine preferred action plan

A decision is not valued until it has been put into effect. The moment it has to be converted into an action plan will provide the true test of your problem-solving process. Sometimes, as social workers and managers, we are faced with having to make decisions that are not 'ideal', perhaps because the problem is so complex, or resources to meet or assess needs are not available. The 'fullest extent' within available resources may be the best that can be achieved. The mark of a good social worker and manager is 'flair' and determination to explore creative alternatives. Always look for several solutions, it is easier than looking for the one.

9. Implement and evaluate

Consider:

- How well did it work?
- What could have led to a better outcome?
- What else needs to be done?
- How far did the solution meet the task requirements or the needs of the service user?
- What did this tell you about your performance?

Towards becoming more creative

Creativity is the application of imaginative thought which results in innovative solutions to problems. We have to rely on habits and routines up to a point – we would really struggle to deal with our day-to-day demands if we had to 'reinvent the wheel' every time we tried to move forward. However, creativity tends to suffer when we rely too heavily on routine and over-restrictive habits. While one purpose of organisational policies and procedures is to achieve structure and consistency, they can also serve to discourage creativity. Policies and creativity should not be regarded as mutually exclusive and the major part of being creative is to break free from such preconceived notions and look at problems through 'a fresh pair of eyes'.

If partnership is to be more than empty rhetoric, we should be working with service users and carers in order to encourage and facilitate creativity with all parties contributing towards breaking down the restrictive barriers of habit and routine (Thompson, 2000). Creative social workers have a talent for getting to the heart of a problem. They are not confused by detail and by the need to evoke standard approaches.

Innovation can be described as the process whereby creative thought develops into something tangible. Creative people are seen as people who generate ideas whereas the innovative process will take those ideas and apply a practical application that is needed or desired within the organisation.

Kanter (1983) argues that:

Innovation is the generation, acceptance and implementation of new ideas, processes, products or services . . . Application and implementation are central to this definition . . . individuals initiate . . . and then work through teams to bring ideas through to innovation.

As we have argued throughout this book, public organisations are different from private sector providers in that they do not produce goods and do not, as a rule, create profit from selling a product. They have different stakeholders and different demands. Therefore, one might ask why we need to be innovative in the public sector.

Currently, the government is a significant driver towards promoting innovation in the public sector. The discussion paper by Mulgan and Albury (2003: 2) states:

Innovation should be a core activity of the public sector: it helps public services to improve performance and increase public value; responds to expectations of citizens and adapts to the needs of users; increases service efficiency and minimise costs . . . How to seek out and foster innovation from all levels is crucial to continual development and improvement.

Mulgan and Albury (ibid.) define innovation as:

The creation and implementation of new processes, products, services and methods of delivery which result in significant improvements in outcomes, efficiency, effectiveness or quality.

Historically, within private sector organisations, a top-down culture has existed. Managers have the 'vision' which is then implemented by the workforce. Research, however, indicates that a significant number of innovative ideas are generated from the bottom-up. It could be argued that this is even more so within a public organisation because front-line practitioners work with service users every day. From your own experiences of implementing policies and procedures within your place of work you might have thought 'It would be much easier or more beneficial to the service user if we could do this differently'. Listening to service users and engaging them in thinking creatively about what they want is crucial.

Barriers towards creativity and innovation

Just as an organisation's environment can foster creative and innovative practices, so can it put up barriers. There is a wealth of work within the field of creativity which is devoted to developing techniques for overcoming the blocks or barriers which tend to get in the way of creating new ideas – the majority of which is written and researched from a private sector perspective. However, the overarching messages remain the same for a public or 'not for profit' organisation:

- No incentives or rewards to innovate or adopt innovations- therefore no motivation to even think about changing anything.
- Short-term budgets and planning horizons – an organisation not valuing innovation and therefore not putting it high on the spending agenda.
- Technologies available but constraining cultural or organisational arrangements.
- Delivery pressures and administrative burdens – workers too 'bogged down' to have the time to be reflective and think creatively.
- Culture of risk aversion – fear of doing things differently.
- Poor teamwork and inadequate management which may lead to apathy and unclear aims and focus.

Smale (1998: 18) outlines the responses that he received from managers when discussing the introduction of innovative management within some local authorities, 'I'd really like to but . . .' or other comments such as:

- It won't work.
- That's a silly idea.
- Is there another time to do this given other work pressures?
- I don't think senior managers will agree.

Consider the following:

Creative people	Blockers
Seek originality	Always do the same thing
Do not follow the crowd	Rely on 'yesterdays' approach
Are unafraid to express new ideas	Fear getting it wrong
Have insight	Lack of motivation
Are not influenced by others	Have the mindsets of others
Have courage	Use organisational constraints

Activity 6.5
- Give your team colleagues a specific time to generate five to ten solutions to a problem.
- Invite each team member to read out one solution until all ideas are presented.
- Members must not judge the appropriateness of any alternative.
- Welcome ideas, even ones that are clearly not going to work.
- Use a yellow stick-it paper to write out each alternative.

- Give each member time to state an alternative – no one is permitted to criticise or dismiss any alternative – even bizarre alternatives can generate realistic alternatives later.
- While one person reads out an idea, others may come up with new ideas.
- Group the ideas into categories.
- Each participant to write out their top five alternatives.
- Group everyone's top five alternatives and begin to combine similar ones.
- Choose the alternatives which are most popular.
- Return to the groupings, and to the group contents separately.
- Prepare list of chosen alternatives.
- Assess each and prepare your action plan.

Activity 6.6
Identify a complex, work-related problem and with the help of your team colleagues apply creative techniques to explore potential solutions.

Making decisions

We turn next to consider professional decision-making and how social workers and managers process and use the information they gather. Decision-making is a key feature of social work and of social work management practice. It includes referral, planning, investigation, assessment, care planning, reviewing, commissioning and closure decisions.

Successful practice relies on responding to presenting problems and the changing nature of the service user's life situation. This involves clarification of objectives, specification of problems and the search for, and implementation of, solutions. Rarely does social work function in ideal situations and decisions are often problematic balancing acts, based on incomplete information, within time constraints, under pressure, with varying degrees of uncertainty as to the likely outcome. Another strand to this is one that emphasises service users as decision-makers with rights to determine their own future. Each of these views forms an integral part of social work practice which recognises that social workers and managers work in a world of uncertainty about which they need to make professional judgements. However, social workers and managers, as we identified in previous chapters, are also regulated by laws, official guidance and procedures.

The nature of presenting problems can mean that, very often, decision-making is the achievement of satisfactory, rather than optimal, results in problem-solving. Professionals may also find themselves having to adopt an economic model of decision-making, which is not based on choice between alternatives, but rather is based on the need to remain focussed on limited constraints and limited resources. All of these factors contribute to the problematic nature of decision-making, but all involve the process of making a choice. So, we can say that decision-making occurs where there is a need or a desire to make a choice (O'Sullivan, 1999). The social workers, or managers, involvement in this activity can take a number of different forms, depending on the decision situation.

The practitioner's role in decision-making

- Making professional judgements.
- Being aware of organisational policies and procedures.
- Supporting, enabling, and facilitating service users' decision-making, in partnership with other agencies and colleagues.
- Making recommendations to others, including higher management, panels and other agencies.
- Knowing about ethical dilemmas and conflicts and how they arise.
- Being aware of values and staying true to them.

An effective decision is one that achieves the required goals but, given the complex nature and uncertainties of service users' situations and the finite nature of resources, this often cannot be certain. The best decision then may be one taken having regard to all of the particular circumstances. Not making a decision is a decision not to act and doing nothing is rarely an option in social work.

One way of making the complexities of social work more manageable, without distorting the work with service users by artificially simplifying it, is to develop a framework to guide you through the steps:

Do:

- Make decisions as you go along – do not let them accumulate. A backlog of many little decisions could be harder to deal with than one big and complex decision.
- Always consider how the decision is to be implemented.
- Before implementing what appears to be the best choice, assess the risk by asking 'What can I think of which might go wrong?'
- Determine when and how the decision is to be renewed – for example, is there a legal requirement?

Once you have made the decision, carry it out with conviction, and trust yourself to defend the consequences appropriately. Most importantly, do not make decisions that are not yours to make.

Decision-making guidelines

What is the problem?

- What evidence of the problem exists?
- What further information do I need to clarify the problem? (make notes and keep your ideas visible so you can consider the relevant information).

What is the purpose?

- What do we want to achieve?
- What are the broad objectives?
- What are the pros and cons of a line of action? (write them down – it clarifies your thinking).

What is the legal context?

- What powers exist?
- What duties exist?
- What are the grounds for intervention?

Who needs to be involved?

- Service users and carers
- Other agencies
- Other stakeholders

What resources?

- What resources do we have?
- What solutions have been tried already?
- Consider those affected by your decision and whenever feasible get them involved.

> **Activity 6.7**
> Using the key points identified above reflect on a case, team or organisational situation where clear decision-making was necessary. Make brief notes to show how you could apply the decision-making guidelines to your work with this situation.

The importance of objectives

In all areas of practice, including problem-solving and decision-making, objectives set out specifically the aims to be achieved and the desired outcomes. Objectives are also an important process involving future courses of action as they:

- Provide a basis for service planning.
- Provide guidelines for decision-making and justification for actions taken.
- Reduce uncertainty in decision-making and give a defence against possible criticism.
- Develop commitment between professionals about what needs to be achieved.
- Develop partnership working.

- Provide standards of performance.
- Provide goals which serve as a basis for the evaluation of change.

In setting objectives, clarity, specificity and simplicity are essential. For the service user the process creates expectations but, sometimes for reasons outside the control of the professionals, jointly agreed objectives cannot be achieved because resources are unavailable, or progress is diverted off course by a range of other factors affecting the lives of service users. Just as assessment is acknowledged as an on-going process, setting objectives should also be regarded in a similar way, not set in tablets of stone, but with flexibility to modify and adapt to changing circumstances. Rarely is there only one approach to addressing assessed need and, if for whatever reason, original objectives cannot be met, problem solving, creativity and innovation are required in the search for alternative approaches. These skills are facets of performance management just as they are practices that contribute to professional effectiveness.

CHAPTER 7

Personal and Professional Development

Key themes in this chapter include:
Communication
Supervision
Motivation
Continual professional development

Introduction

A manager may acquire the theoretical knowledge at a strategic and operational level in order to be efficient and effective, but, without the support of people who make up teams or organisations very little is achievable. Coercive power may persuade some staff members to 'go along' with change initiatives but 'go along' is perhaps all that they will do and no more. Coercive power can breed resentment and is not sustainable for any length of time and many organisations, especially those who deliver social care, rely on the goodwill of their staff members to get by from day to day. Eventually, if people are not satisfied with what is going on around them, staff retention will suffer and those with a wealth of concrete and tacit knowledge, information and skill, will leave the organisation.

As social care managers we can all recall the sinking feeling when one of our most experienced social workers announces they are leaving the team and we know there is no one in the short term who has the experience to step into the job. There are cases to reallocate, rotas to fill, perhaps court dates and service user reviews to cover for leaving colleagues and, as we have noted previously, deadlines to meet and a quality of service to be maintained. For the service user this invariably means another social worker, new relationships and trust to build, information to retell and perhaps no service or support at all until a replacement is found. It is no wonder that managers have sought help from agency staff because they can fill the gap quickly whilst the process of recruitment of permanent staff takes place. Clearly, no-one would deny that safety is paramount and that recruitment procedures need to be stringent and rigorous. Nevertheless, for all stakeholders, the recruitment process can seem slow and arduous.

Activity 7.1

Eleanor, the most experienced senior practitioner in the team, has just told you that she will be leaving after she has worked her two months notice. She has been successful in gaining promotion so there is no option of negotiation. You know that she works with some of the most challenging service users but you have two months to plan with her to ensure the smooth transfer of her workload to other staff members of the team. The only problem is that the team is already short staffed and those in the team also have a full workload. As the team manager what actions would you take over the next two months to ensure that Eleanor's service users are not left without a social worker when she leaves?

For a team to be effective and efficient within a changing environment there is a need for stability or low turnover of staff within the team or organisation. Stability assists teams to grow and develop together and embeds knowledge and information. How does the team manager achieve this when the team is made up of social workers who can leave and easily move on to other teams and organisations because demand for qualified social workers is outstripping supply? Clearly, in the scenario outlined in Activity 7.1 the staff member is leaving due to promotion, and as team managers we would not wish to stand in the way of other people's careers. However, other staff members may leave for a multitude of reasons that can be avoided. As the Audit Commission (2002: 4) argue, public sector managers are pivotal to recruitment and retention strategies because:

Most public sector staff are leaving because of push, not pull factors. Many of the critical short, and medium term solutions can be delivered at local level, and leadership and management are crucial since the right solutions are not stand alone fixes that can be left to human resources directorates. Instead they lie at the heart of how organisations are managed and led.

The Audit Commission suggests that there are four critical factors that are at the root of successful recruitment and retention of staff:

- People's experience of work must match their expectations.
- The work environment must engage, enable and support staff to make a positive difference to service users and local communities.
- Those delivering public services must feel that they are valued, respected and fairly rewarded.
- The shift from a public sector to a private service workforce must be actively managed to create a synergy, rather than a clash of values.

Communicating the vision

As Grant (1995: 126) aptly notes, organisations are increasingly recognising that in evaluating their human resources it is not just individuals' expertise and knowledge that is important but also their ability to work effectively together. This must be true across teams and professional groups but, equally, vertically within the hierarchy of organisations.

We have all heard the phrase 'taking people along with you', and as a manager this is exactly what is necessary. Staff members within the team or organisation need to be able to see where the organisation is going from both a macro and a micro perspective. They need to feel a valued part of the organisation and involved in and consulted about any changes that are being implemented. Staff members also need to understand the relevance and impact of what is going on around them in relation to their own identity, their role and responsibilities, and their practice setting, and also how change will affect their work with service users. In many instances, staff members become de-motivated and disinterested in what is going on around them because the manager or organisation does not convey the feeling of valuing their staff or is inept at sharing appropriate information. As we have noted in previous chapters, part of a team's or organisation's culture arises from myths and stories and these can abound if staff members hear fragments of information. It is common to speculate or finish the story from a pessimistic perspective with devastating consequences for staff morale and motivation. A manager may have the intention of valuing and including their staff group but without communicating that intention staff will not know and fear the worst.

Many organisations use a mission or vision statement as a form of communicating their overarching purpose to their various stakeholders. Zaccaro and Banks (2001: 184) provide common definitions which we can adapt to a service sector:

- Visions provide a representation of what the organisation is striving to become i.e. a quality service, providing value for money, efficient, effective.
- Visions reflect values i.e. working together with service users, being respectful, being transparent.
- Visions are symbols of change which bring all members of the organisation together as a collective whole. As such, they give meaning and inspiration to the workforce.

Activity 7.2

Consider your own organisation's vision or mission statement. How accurately does this statement reflect what is going on within your organisation. Does it convey the nature and direction of your organisation? Does it reflect the values of your profession and service? Does it help to give meaning or inspiration to the workforce? Does it explicitly include the voice of service users and carers? Write a mission or vision statement which you feel accurately portrays the organisation or team that you manage.

Communication

From a practice perspective, effective communication within the social work and social care arena is paramount. Indeed, as O'Connor et al. point out (2006: 59):

> While many of the communication skills we use in social work practice are used in everyday life, it is particularly important that social workers understand these skills and how they can be used to assist others. Being able to describe to service users, to supervisors, or to co-workers what you are doing is an essential ingredient in being able to account for your intervention.

From a manager's perspective, good communication skills are vital in order to ensure that practice is safe and conforms to policies and procedures and that team or organisational goals are clear.

The Department for Education and Skills highlight communication in their document, *Common Core Skills and Knowledge for the Children's Workforce: Every Child Matters, Change for Children* (2005: 4) which states that:

> Good communication is central to working with children, young people, their families and carers. It is a fundamental part of the Common Core. It involves listening, questioning, understanding and responding to what is being communicated by children, young people and those caring for them . . . Communication is not just about the words you use, but also your manner of speaking, body language and, above all, the effectiveness with which you listen. To communicate effectively it is important to take into account culture and context, for example where English is an additional language.

Mintzberg (1991) undertook research into what managers actually do in their role and found that engaging in ad hoc communication was how most managers spent most of their time. Consider the various people that a manager might communicate with in the course of their working week:

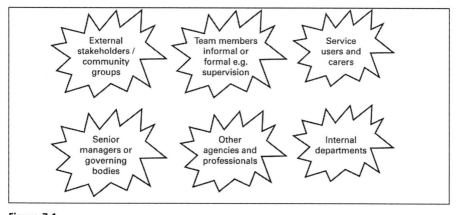

Figure 7.1

Activity 7.3

Think of your current role and complete a diagram similar to Figure 7.1. Taking each of the groups of people identified, consider what proportion of your working week is spent communicating with individuals, departments or agencies.

- What form does your communication take – verbal, non-verbal, reflective, electronic, face-to-face?
- What method is the most effective?
- Is this the same for all the stakeholders you have identified?

Miller (2002: 19) offers the following guidance to consider when faced with confusion, low morale and resistance, and where communication is seen to be the problem through lack of clarity, lack of sufficient communication, lack of two-way communication:

Lack of clarity: Does the organisation or team really hear what the key messages or mission is? The manager needs to reflect back on what the organisation is hearing by asking people what they understand as the main goals and key issues. Are the key messages comprehensible and are they actually well-articulated at senior management levels;

Lack of sufficient communication: Are managers using every channel at their disposal to communicate key messages effectively. For example, managers might wish to use one communication outlet such as the internet, but if the majority of workers do not turn on their computer each day then this is not going to be effective. Managers, therefore, need to know their staff and know their work patterns and habits. There are many other forms of outlets for communication such as newsletters, story boards, team meetings, organisation briefing sessions and conferences, and it may be more effective to use several different means;

Lack of two-way communication: There may be a great deal of one-way communication, perhaps from the top-down within the organisation, but one might argue that this is not communication but rather 'directive'.

Activity 7.4

Consider the above barriers that step in the way of effective communication from your perspective and that of your team or organisation. Identify one area or incident where you feel one or more of the above barriers existed. What solutions can be put in place to break down the barriers identified?

Supervision and effective communication

I am more and more convinced that whilst training managers in supervision is neither compulsory or seemingly adequately appreciated in its value, it leaves a void in the potential of managers to be effective in the precise role of managing their staff. Understanding their responsibilities towards their team members and being supported to fulfil those roles could avoid the extent of the apathy, low morale and office politics I have witnessed.

(Qualified social worker, 2006)

The General Social Care Council (2002, para. 2.2) states in their code of practice for employers of social care workers that they must ensure the 'effective managing and supervising of staff to support effective practice and good conduct and supporting staff to address deficiencies in their performance'.

Tsui (2005: 490) argues that supervision is a tool that allows the supervisor to establish a work team and enhance communication and cooperation among the staff. In a study of supervisors and supervisees working in Hong Kong, Tsui concluded that, 'supervision is a means to communicate, co-ordinate and co-operate with one another as a team'.

As Beckett (2006: 194) states:

Put at its most simplest, social work supervision consists of a period of time in which a social worker, or sometimes a group of social workers, discuss their work with someone else. Typically in social work this is with the social worker's immediate line manager.

But what really does take place when the office door is closed for that hour or two? How structured is it? How consistent is it? How motivational is it? How effective is it?

Supervision should not be a monologue but rather a purposeful dialogue between two people where knowledge and information is shared, discussed and challenged. As part of his or her duties and responsibilities, the team manager is accountable for ensuring that every person within the team has supervision at a frequency determined by the organisation's policy and procedures. More frequently than that specified may depend on the supervisee's individual circumstances i.e. new members of staff, students, staff members experiencing particular difficulties or staff where it has been identified that performance needs monitoring more frequently.

The sharing and discussion of knowledge and information has the primary objective of ensuring that practice is safe and well informed. Indeed, Lord Laming states (2003: para. 6.638): 'Effective supervision is the cornerstone of safe social work practice'. As such, the barriers to effective and safe practice must also form part of the supervision session as they arise. These barriers may include training needs, personal development, team dynamics, sickness and health and safety, motivation, time and workload management, poor practice issues and any other difficulties. Skills for Care (2006, p. 14) point out that the emphasis on supervision, accountability, appraisal and staff development are a key role across all levels.

What is effective supervision?

The Laming Inquiry (2003: para. 6.630) identified some key features of effective supervision and notes that it should be:

> . . . *well documented and should include discussion of individual cases and opportunity to challenge assumptions and judgements that have been made regarding particular cases and to agree plans of action* . . .

and (recommendation 45):

> *Directors of social services must ensure that the work of staff working directly with children is regularly supervised. This must include the supervisor reading, reviewing and signing the case file at regular intervals.*

and (recommendation 53):

> *When allocating a case to a social worker, the manager must ensure that the social worker is clear as to what has been allocated, what action is required and how that action will be reviewed and supervised.*

Supervision records are the cornerstone to safe practice and all supervision sessions must be recorded. Commonly, the recording of a supervision session should contain two distinct elements – one relating specifically to issues that pertain to the supervisee and the other relating specifically to casework. Turner (2000: 233) and Kadushin (1976) make reference to social work supervision having three primary functions, namely administration, education and support.

> ### Activity 7.5
> Consider Figure 7.2 which outlines some key elements of supervision. What ones would you consider to be administrative, what ones relate to education or development and what ones directly relate to support. Where is the emphasis? Is this emphasis appropriate?

Turner (2006: 238) asked social workers, first-line managers, staff development officers and senior managers for their views on the functions of supervision in their agencies and found that organisations are beginning to experiment with new systems for supervising social workers, and that some are separating the tasks associated with the supervision of practice from other managerial responsibilities. Indeed, some organisations have created a position of 'practice manager' to oversee and supervise the casework element which then leaves the manager to focus on a more strategic view such as the overall effectiveness and motivation of the team.

Motivating the team

As Gill argues (2006: 231) leadership is most commonly associated with influencing, motivating and inspiring people to want to do what needs to be done. Gill further argues that inspiration and passion are inextricably interlinked.

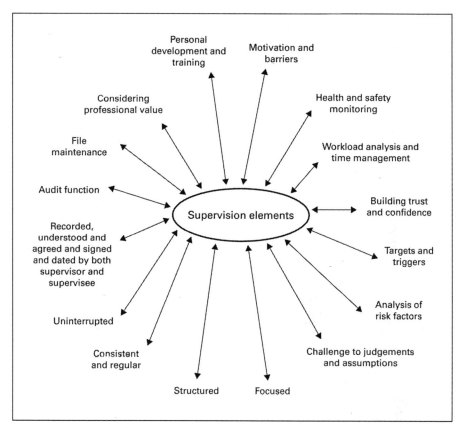

Supervision elements

- Personal development and training
- Motivation and barriers
- Considering professional value
- Health and safety monitoring
- File maintenance
- Workload analysis and time management
- Audit function
- Building trust and confidence
- Recorded, understood and agreed and signed and dated by both supervisor and supervisee
- Targets and triggers
- Uninterrupted
- Analysis of risk factors
- Consistent and regular
- Challenge to judgements and assumptions
- Structured
- Focused

Figure 7.2

Komisar (2002, cited in Gill, 2006: 232), offers us a definition, although looking from a business perspective, that we can apply to the social care sector:

Passion is what individuals care about, what difference they hope to make, what constructive change they propose to lead. Passion is an undeniable force generated from within . . . When I find passion aligned with vision, I know the venture is authentic . . . the real secret to reawakening passion in one's work is integrating what we do with who we are.

Motivation is a 'driving force' through which people strive to achieve their goals and fulfil some need to uphold their values (Mullins, 1993). Figure 7.3 offers us a way of considering how motivation fits within this framework (Locke and Henne, 1986).

As social work practitioners you may work with adults or families where there is a great need to change and where specific needs have been identified through

Figure 7.3

the assessment process. Being mindful of your professional value base you may work with the service user to reach common and achievable goals which can create the desired change. However, there is a need to motivate the service user to change for without this there is a likelihood that there will be little sustainable action.

Activity 7.6
- As managers, how do we influence, motivate and inspire our team?
- Using the outline in Figure 7.3 what tools and strategies do you adopt?
- How effective are they?
- What outcomes have you seen from your efforts to motivate your team or organisation?

From a psychological perspective, motivation arises from both internal and external influences. By the same token, the motivated individual or team can become de-motivated without good leadership or in times of change if there is, for example, role confusion or role ambiguity.

Maslow (1970) suggested five hierarchical levels of need which influence an individual's behaviour:

- Physiological needs – the need for food, shelter.
- Safety needs – protection against danger or risk.
- Needs to belong – the need for belonging, acceptance, friendship.
- Self-esteem needs – the need for reputation, status.
- Self-actualisation – the need to realise one's own potential for continual self-development.

As social work managers, it is important to revisit Maslow's hierarchy in relation to the staff group. Clearly, the most optimal level for all staff is one of self-actualisation but how many are stuck below this level and at what cost to themselves and their service user group?

Clearly, people are motivated by different factors, some of which may be intrinsic and come from within, whilst others are extrinsic, such as monetary rewards. It has long been argued that people who work in the caring professions are motivated by intrinsic rewards. The goal setting theory of motivation, (Mullins, 1993), argues that people set their goals and attempt to achieve them in a manner that is consistent with their needs and values. Social workers set themselves professional goals: for example, to ensure the safety of vulnerable people; to work to ensure social inclusion; to keep families together or to help elderly people achieve a quality of life within the community. Consider Figure 7.4:

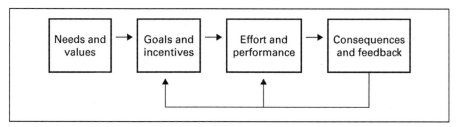

Figure 7.4

An individual might consider a career as a social care worker because of the needs and values they have; they qualify and join a team with certain goals, perhaps to support people with learning difficulties to live independently within the community, and they might put a great deal of effort into achieving this. Their effort arises from the motivation to succeed and achieve their goal and may take many forms, for example, further training or taking on more complex work to gain further experience. Perhaps the outcome of their work results in the person with learning difficulties being unable to live in the community because of a lack of sufficient community base resources or funding. Perhaps the social worker will revisit the goals and effort, but, if the outcome remains the same, it is likely to have a detrimental effect on their motivation.

Activity 7.7
- If you were this social worker's manager how would you try to ensure that they remained motivated?
- From an organisation perspective, how useful is it to consider goal setting theory as a management tool to promote team motivation?
- Think of two areas where you can apply this to your team.

Summary
This chapter has considered some aspects of managing the staff group. We have argued that the people who make up teams and organisations are the key to the team's success. Optimally, the most successful teams are those who can recruit and retain their staff members, for stability is the basis for increased knowledge and experience. Increased knowledge and experience has a direct effect on the quality of service that is provided. A knowledgeable and experienced social worker knows their community, knows the professional

networks, has experience of working across established professional boundaries, has built up trusting professional relationships and perhaps knows the service user or their family members. They also know the infrastructure and the procedures and can act more efficiently when the need arises. They have also formed good peer group support networks within their team.

The social care manager plays a vital role in ensuring that staff do not leave the organisation. We have highlighted some important areas that managers must consider in order to retain, value, support and motivate their staff group. As one newly qualified social worker remarked:

I think they need to maintain loyalty to their staff and stability in their team, while facing the conflicts that inevitably arise. I think being approachable is very important. They might be doing some great work, but, if they are hiding away in their office their team is not being supported.

(Qualified social worker, 2006)

CHAPTER 8

The Influence of Self: Towards a New Reality?

Key themes in this chapter include:
Changing worlds
Community anchors
Thematic hubs
Different practice settings
Value base

Introduction

Our discussion so far has been concerned with introducing a theoretical and practical approach to understanding the changing role of the social worker and manager. We have identified a number of managerial, cultural and environmental influences and in this chapter we build on that understanding and consider what needs to change. We present the changing nature of social work as a challenge to re-establish the value base and transfer the knowledge and skills of practice and management to a variety of different settings. Far from being a pessimistic conclusion this chapter recognises the opportunity waiting to happen for social work and social care practitioners and managers as a contribution to the future policy debate.

The influence of self: towards a new reality?

I had a discussion with the service manager about staying in touch with reality as the social problems faced by our service users seem to intensify or change over the years and the changing ethnic diversity of the locality. She now takes on one day of duty a month and carries out full assessments. This seems to have had a positive effect on the team as the feeling is she can understand and empathise with their role conflicts and work experiences in a much more current way and at the same level rather than an outdated, unrealistic attitude towards time management and information gathering.

(Qualified social worker, 2006)

Despite pleas to adopt a more preventative approach to services there has been a marked reluctance to do so which is in part explained by economic factors but also by emerging questions of social work effectiveness. Indeed, such doubts, as we discussed in previous chapters, led both Conservative (1979) and Labour (1997) governments to the view that the remedy was to bring market forces to bear on social care.

What was once a debate between individual casework and community empowerment has become one of care and case management. Social work as a profession has now merged, some might say confusingly, with social care and it is becoming more difficult to say what a social worker is. In Chapter 7 we discussed role confusion and role ambiguity as factors which decrease motivation that, in times of change, is vital for successful practice. There is now a widely held perception that social work will be 'taken away' from local councils and swallowed up by its powerful neighbours in health and education. A number of key reform proposals add weight to this view, not least the government's enthusiasm for closer structural ties between health and social care within adult services, and between social work and education for work with children and families. Further, reform of social care is routinely included as part of National Health Service plans.

The concept of a single organisation, however, has implications for some form of joint management and despite the promotion in the White Paper, *Our Health, Our Care, Our Say* (2006) of more integrated services there remain, as we have previously argued, organisational, cultural and professional differences to be addressed. In the absence of clear evidence as to whether health and social care or education and social care are better integrated in order to ensure that service users receive a better service remains to be evaluated. However, the risk of creating an expanded bureaucracy may lead instead to a variety of different models of integrated working that results in confusion for all the professional workers involved.

What is clear is that social work as a profession has been significantly affected as local authority departments have become subservient to the interests of education and health care. For some that may be a cause for regret and reflection, whilst for others there is true recognition and opportunity for social workers to offer a distinctive set of knowledge, skills, values and passions towards supporting the most vulnerable people in our society. We would argue that is more important than a debate about where practice should be located. **The fear that social work will become part of health or education perpetuates a misunderstanding of what social workers have to offer in a wider social context as social entrepreneurs, working with and on behalf of people who need help to improve their quality of life.** We will return later in this chapter to consider these opportunities.

The strength of concern for the demise of social service departments should not, however, be forgotten. While there is much to commend the spread of professional practice within a broader social context, it can be argued that the loss of democratic control is too important to abandon without a fight. The link between voters, councillors and social workers is very important and needs to be valued and strengthened. There is after all, no equivalent pathway in the National Health Service.

At best these arguments are overstated, after all, local and central government funding has done little to ease the mounting pressures on delivery of local social care services. The emerging consequence is that, increasingly, social workers are operating in a climate dictated by scarcity of resources, demand for tight control of budgets, strict eligibility criteria, high caseloads and maximum outcomes. Social workers find themselves rationing services to save money which, coupled with a tendency to over bureaucratise for past failings and obsession with targets rather than good outcomes for service users, has left social workers lamenting the decline of basic skills in making relationships with service users. We would argue that this latter point should be at the heart of social work practice.

The development of care management with its characteristic 'tick box mentality' has gone hand-in-hand with overriding budgetary pressures and consequent service delivery rather than a practice based on forming therapeutic relationships. This has had an undermining influence on the way social workers perceive their roles and the way their skills are valued. Many social workers, Payne suggests (2006) are despondent about the future of social work and believe that it has become a divided, de-professionalised and discredited profession. Where once social work was recognised as the central task of a major public service it has now dwindled down to the rationing role of care and case management. Social workers have been restricted to administering a set of social care services bound up with risk assessment and service delivery. Social work, it could be argued, has come to be seen as more authoritarian as a result of this rigidity and this has become the defining identity for social workers in the public eye. We might conclude that the practising professional, using therapeutic skills and direct one-to-one intervention with service users, is fast becoming a rarity.

The temptation to regard the introduction of managerialism, quasi-markets (Chapter 2) and performance management (Chapter 6) as being in some way to blame for the current ills of social work, may for some be compelling but these ideas are not in themselves new. They do, however, challenge the traditional culture of public services, particularly for those ideologically at variance with policies that expand the independent sector delivery of care services. There is concern that public money is employed to purchase services from private organisations and businesses which are run for profit; money that could otherwise be spent in public service provision that has no monetary profit element and might therefore be expected to make a wider contribution to meeting need. The difficulty with this approach is the reality of central and local government funding pressures, which along with escalating service demand, points to further drives to achieve efficiency savings and a promotion of greater self-responsibility.

In defence of the government, Henwood (2006) argues that New Labour wants to transform public services by reducing top-down command and control management and ending the monolithic approach to services in favour of devolved power and autonomy to innovate at local level. This theme is reflected in central and local government initiatives that refer to 'promoting choice', 'independence', 'health' and 'social inclusion' and approaches that 'put power in the hands of the patient, the parent and citizen' (Labour Party Manifesto, 2005: 5). Whether these policy aspirations reflect an agenda of cost reduction on the one hand, or enhancement of service user empowerment on the other, is a matter of opinion, although arguably both have a place and should not be regarded as mutually exclusive objectives. It is, however, the fear of privatisation that has become a major stumbling block to dealing with the heart of what needs to change, structurally and organisationally, in order to revitalise and refocus services on the core values of social work.

The real challenge for social workers and managers is not to emulate the more negative and distorted stereotypes of the private business world, but rather to absorb those ideas which suggest that success lies in valuing, fostering and listening to the workforce, hearing and responding to the 'customer', managing diversity not conformity and seeking to build flexibility at every stage (Coulshed and Mullender, 2006: 221) So what does this mean in practice?

Changing 'worlds'

Strategic managers work in a 'management world' where they process copious amounts of knowledge, interpret data, processes and policies in, and for, an organisation. There is a tendency in social work to increasingly gather information as a means of meeting government expectations in relation to performance and change management, but the data collected appears to more readily reflect the management of data collection rather than the characteristics of the entries measured. Data collected during periods of applying coping mechanisms, Wolstenholme (2006) argues, reflect nothing more than overload and bear no relationship to the impact on people and the service provided.

In this 'world', the gap between strategic management and professional practice can easily become a chasm in which shared purpose, values and objectives become lost because the organisation loses sight of 'the business we are in'. The 'worlds' of management and practice risk growing apart if social work values are sacrificed to the managerialist agenda. This implies a need for a change in organisational culture to one that promotes the importance of values and practice-led approaches to management, and that builds bridges between professional and management issues (Statham, 1996).

We have argued that many local authority departments operate with a culture of survival where they have to be seen to meet political and community expectations (Chapter 4). To expect more from fixed resources consigns professional roles to managing access to existing services, rather than helping people find solutions to their problems. The question remains about where social work is positioned in this climate of change. Jordan and Jordan (2000: 37) ask:

> . . . *whether professional social work any longer seeks to be credible at street level, with service users and carers, or whether it is developing into an arms length, office bound report writing official kind of practice, which leaves face-to-face work to others.*

Every social worker is having to learn new management skills and approaches but the burden of organisationally imposed administrative functions may be becoming the centrality of the professional task. Yet for all this, social work is not a bureaucratic endeavour, but one in which creativity is constantly required to think out new solutions and approaches to new and old problems. What this means in the current context is a need to look for the kind of management leadership that can change attitudes, traditional ways of working and relationships, into an alternative model that moves away from a simplistic (although made all too often complex) divide between manager and professional (Causer and Exworthy, 1999). In Chapter 2 we showed how Rajan (2000) captures the essence of leadership in terms of its transformational nature and ability to make sense of complexity in an atmosphere of exceptional ambiguity.

Reflecting on the future

The next phase of social work development, Payne (2006) suggests, is going to be the creation of a range of different social professions, a collection of social workers (note the plural) co-ordinated not by administrative structures but by shared professional knowledge and skills. Social work, Payne believes, will be the stronger for not relying on local government structures for its identity. A view we share. So what then are the implications for professional roles and identity? In Chapter 2 we have argued that social workers currently undertake a range of management functions with every professional decision having a budgetary implication. This may be so, but professional identity needs a more profound conceptual framework rather than merely adding in specific managerial skills.

The Government's political agenda points clearly to a belief in the development of specialist approaches to service delivery and these centrally-driven changes suggest that tomorrow's social work will be practised in a variety of settings. Far from being a threat to professional identity, new settings and approaches to governance provide the opportunity to draw on genuine social work skills. Greater autonomy within accountability frameworks will mean that social workers are required to explain and account for their practice in basing decisions and planning their actions on sound assessment and on robust evidence of what works. It calls for enhanced problem solving and decision making skills, backed up by sound judgement and best practice.

Tomorrow's social worker does not need to be a 'strongly bonded individual with a sense of self apart from others' but, instead, someone who values and connects with others, using the multiplicity of experiences of service users and team members to develop adaptive and creative solutions. With this approach, it is not so much what the individual social worker can do but what the social worker working with others can become. Consider the following points that could constitute a new professional identity:

Characteristics of a new professional identity
- Reflective application of knowledge: Integrating knowledge and experience in a specific service context.
- A strong sense of self in connection with others.
- Team player: Welcoming and valuing the contribution of others.
- Acknowledging the unique expertise and experience of all.
- Networker: identifying and utilising team member's experience as a resource for service users.
- Integrated whole system approach to practice and management.
- Continual professional development.

Neighbourhood approach

While the context of social work is constantly changing it continues to remain concerned with some of the most complex and disturbing problems of human experience. Much of what social workers do is rooted in disadvantage, oppression and discrimination as they attempt to help service users face uncertainties, apprehension and fears of change (Chapter 1).

Jordan (1997) notes the absence of social work amongst non-westernised societies. So what is it about the modern western free market democracies that produces a demand for social work?

Development of western social democratic capitalist societies is based on a model of freedom to make choices and it follows that if people and carers fail to exercise their freedoms in the best interest of those who are most vulnerable then the state has a choice either to intervene or to do nothing (Horner, 2003). A third choice is to engage with potentially vulnerable individuals and groups in the community by working with them to address the causes of their difficulties. While the historical emergence of social work falls outside the scope of our discussion, community work has always been an important facet of social work intervention. Yet, like other areas of public service, social work is failing to connect with people. The inability of different social care organisations, public and voluntary, to talk to one another is the reason the government cites as a key cause for individuals to slip through the social safety net. This is a feeling reflected in 'New Deal for Communities' which aims to improve social and environmental conditions by bringing together relevant organisations.

This is not to suggest that communities are to be respected and preserved simply by virtue of their being a community and it is possible that enthusiasm for 'community' is a kind of nostalgia. We have heard stories from the East End of London and the Valleys of Wales about never having to lock doors and 'community spirit'. Communitarianism may at first reading appear attractive and this is perhaps one reason why the government endorses it as a core value. However, the promotion of community, Giddens (1998, p. 79) suggests, does not imply trying to recapture lost forms of community spirit and solidarity but is a practical means of furthering the social and material refurbishment of neighbourhoods.

The social principles espoused by the Labour Government owe much to the works of communitarian thinkers and stress in particular the ideas of duty and responsibility. While we do not doubt the importance of these virtues, we first need a renewed recognition of and investment in communities, as vital units of social organisation, which will add to the significance of community care. Importantly, it provides a means of enhancing local agencies and encouraging greater use of independent organisations in both voluntary and commercial sectors through an infrastructure which facilitates, enables and encourages individual involvement.

An opportunity waiting to happen?

We have acknowledged the gradual demise of local government and its traditional role in the provision of social care. Perhaps there is a need for local government to determine whether its primary role is that of service provider or one that purely represents the needs of its community. The latter would suggest that its role is one of advocacy and purchasing rather than directly providing services. The question then is how social care services can be provided and by whom?

The notion of 'thematic hubs' and 'community anchors' offer a model for discussion. Consider the diagram below which give an example of the centrality of the multi-professional hub and its surrounding community anchors. Some suggestion has been made relating to how services could be distributed within each anchor. This is not an exhaustive list of services, for example, the voluntary and independent sector could, and is likely to, feature within the multi-professional hub and its anchors.

The number of thematic community anchors needed within one neighbourhood is a matter of debate. A large neighbourhood, for example, may use a model of several community anchors whilst a smaller community may have just one. The essence is that the model allows for flexibility within each community depending on specific demand, need and demographic factors.

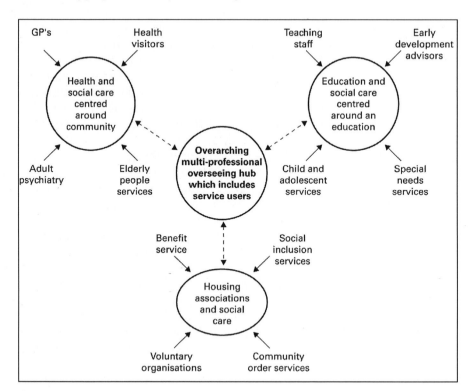

Figure 8.1

Community anchors feature a primary service at the centre of a group of smaller voluntary, community, and where appropriate, public organisations which are connected by a common goal. In some neighbourhoods, for example, housing associations are the strongest and most experienced third sector organisation. The wealth of resources of associations, allied to their experience and local knowledge of community and voluntary organisations, can produce a powerful force for partnership arrangements 'anchored ' in the community by the associations. There are strong ethical arguments in addition to those of efficiency for a common effort both to reduce neighbourhood poverty and to promote effective neighbourhood management.

Community anchors featuring housing associations at the centre might include a common mission to:

- Reduce anti-social behaviour.
- Tackle homelessness.
- Seek accommodation for young people leaving care.
- Promote training initiatives.
- Give advice and debt counselling.

- Promote community safety initiatives.

Community anchors featuring education at the centre might include a common mission to:

- Provide early year education and social care.
- Expand the youth service.
- Promote the use of children centres.
- Provide support for sure start schemes.
- Promote connexions services within the education arena.
- Develop healthy living initiatives.
- Extend school agenda initiatives.

Community anchors featuring health at the centre might include a common mission to:

- Develop appropriate service development across the life span.
- Provide drug and alcohol misuse support.
- Target specific public health issues within the locality.
- Support services to vulnerable people.
- Promote healthy living initiatives.

Each of the primary services act as a community anchor which co-ordinates the range of service providers within the neighbourhood. The idea of community anchors is clearly topical and the government has introduced a number of initiatives to encourage social enterprises and voluntary and community groups to 'grow their businesses'. Increasing third sector involvement opens up new integrated funding sources in addition to those provided by local government commissioning arrangements and central government grant.

This approach recognises the location of statutory work, such as protection, remaining within the structure of local government whilst the overarching thematic hub and community anchors provide opportunities for preventative social work in new multi-disciplinary settings.

Within the proposed model, the central hub might usefully serve as a vehicle for bringing together purchasers and providers in a more integrated and transparent approach to strategic and financial service planning. The central hub also provides a bridge between the community and statutory provision. Thematic hubs are intended to serve local communities and are essentially small, non-hierarchical and community driven. The management for thematic hubs would largely be provided within the primary service organisation in its role as community anchor.

This model offers one way of considering social care in different settings and will hopefully provide a framework for future discussion. The challenge for new forms of governance is to engage practitioners and service users in jointly contributing to the formation of policies and priorities. Experience has shown that the greater the gaps between management and practice, policy and practice, practice and service user the greater is the likelihood that organisational objectives will fail to secure effective service outcomes.

Return to practice

We have discussed the changing role of social work in many contexts but, essentially, we return to what remains at the core of professional practice in all its forms, tasks and settings. The skill to help people is no less complex and, in many ways, it is the most difficult.

When the General Social Care Council announced the reform of social work education, it set up a series of focus groups to ask service users, carers, academics and employers to identify the desired personal characteristics of a social worker. What matters to service users is summarised in two short statements in their report:

- The need for social workers to understand what a person's life is really like, and not to make assumptions and judgements about what they think a person needs.
- The importance of the quality of the relationship that the social worker has with the service user.

These comments highlight the importance of relationships that make a difference to people's lives. Despite the language of managerialism and the importation of quality control mechanisms, Powell (2001: 67) suggests that:

> . . . social work's value system is located in the classical humanist notion of a virtuous society, based upon a commitment to humanity, equality and social justice, rather than the vagaries of fortune that define market capitalism.

Perhaps ultimately it is these enduring values that might prove more resilient than the transient fashions of organisational delivery structures. As Cree summarises (2000: 28):

> Social work has a long tradition of working alongside people, valuing difference and having concern for social justice and inequality. These are the aspects of social work that we must build on in the future wherever social work is located.

The vision of change, whatever the outcome, offers social workers and managers an opportunity to revisit their professional identity and reaffirm the value base of their practice and in this respect change offers an opportunity waiting to happen.

References

Adaire, J. (1984) *Effective Leadership*. Aldershot: Gower.

Adams, K. et al. (2006) Investigating the Factors Influencing Professional Identity of First Year Health and Social Care Students. *Learning in Health and Social Care.* 5: 2, 55–68.

Adams, R. (1998) *Quality Social Work*. Basingstoke: Macmillan.

Adams, R., Dominelli, L. and Payne, M. (2002) *Critical Practice in Social Work*. Basingstoke: Palgrave.

Alder, R.B. and Rodman, G. (1991) *Understanding Human Communication*. Holt, Rhinehart and Winstone: Texas, Lewin.

Arroba, T. and Wedgwood-Oppenheim, F. (1994) Do Senior Managers Differ in Public Sector and Private Sector? An Examination of Team Role Preference. *Journal of Psychology.* 9: 1.

Audit Commission (2002) *Recruitment and Retention: A Public Service Workforce for the 21st Century*. London: Audit Commission.

Audit Commission (2004) *Old Virtues, New Virtues: An Overview of the Changes in Social Care Services Over the Seven Years of Joint Reviews in England 1996–2003*. London: Audit Commission.

Baggini, J. (2000) Target Trouble. *The Stakeholder.* 4: 14–15.

Barney, J.B. (1997) *Gaining and Sustaining Competitive Advantage*. Reading, MA: Addison-Wesley.

Barrett, G., Sellman, D. and Thomas (2005) *Interprofessional Working in Health and Social Care: Professional Perspectives*. Basingstoke: Palgrave.

Batty, D. (2002) Unsocial Services. *Guardian Newspaper*, 15.10.

Beckett, C. (2006) *Essential Theory for Social Work Practice*. London: Sage.

Biestek, F. (1961) *The Casework Relationship*. London: Allen and Urwin.

Blair, T. (1999) Modernising Public Services for Services for Charter Mark Awards. In Audit Commission (2002) *Recruitment and Retention: A Public Service Workforce for the 21st Century*. London: Audit Commission.

Blake, R.R. and Moulton, J.S. (1964) *The Managerial Grid*. Huston: TX Gulf.

Bourne, J. (1979) *Management in Central and Local Government*. London: Pitman.

Bryman, A. (1986) *Charisma and Leadership of Organisations*. London: Sage.

Buchanan, D.A. and Huczynski, A.A. (1985) *Organizational Behaviour: An Introductory Text*. Englewood Cliffs, NJ: Prentice Hall.

Busher, H. (2005) Being a Middle Leader: Exploring Professional Identities. *School Leadership and Management.* 25: 2, 137–53.

Callero, P.L. (1985) Role-Identity Salience. *Social Psychology Quarterly*, 48: 203–15.

Causer, G. and Exworthy, M. (1999) Professionals as Managers Across the Public Sector. In M. Exworthy and S. Halford (eds.) *Professionals and the New Managerislism in the Public Sector*. Buckingham: Open University Press.

CCETSW (1996) *Assuring Quality for the Diploma in Social Work: Rules and Requirements for the DipSW*. CCETSW (2nd revision).

CEML (2002) *Managers and Leaders: Raising Our Game*. www.managementandleadershipcouncil.org

Chartered Institute of Personnel and Development (1999) *Benchmarking for People Managers: A Competence Approach*. London: CIPD.

Clarke, J. and Newman, J. (1997) *The Managerial State: Power, Politics and Ideology in the Remaking of Social Welfare*. London: Sage.

Clough, R. (1998) The Future of Residential Care. In Jack, R. (Ed.) *Residential Versus Community Care*. Basingstoke: Macmillan.

Cohen, H.A. (1981) *The Nurse's Quest for a Professional Identity.* CA: Addison-Wesley.

Couiser, G. and Exworthy, M. (1999) Professionals as Managers Across the Public Sector. In Exworthy, M. and Halford, S. (Eds.) *Professionals and the New Managerialism in the Public Sector.* Buckingham: Open University Press.

Coulshed, V. and Mullender, A. (2006) *Management in Social Work.* 3rd edn. Basingstoke: Palgrave Macmillan/BASW.

Crainer, S. (1998) *Key Management Ideas: Thinkers that Changed the Management World.* 3rd edn. Engelwood Cliffs, NJ: Prentice Hall.

Cree, V. (2002) The Changing Nature of Social Work. In Adams, R., Dominelli, L. and Payne, M. (Eds.) *Critical Practice in Social Work.* Basingstoke: Palgrave.

Davis, M. (1997) *Companion to Social Work.* Oxford: Blackwell.

Deal, T.E. and Kennedy, A.A. (1982) *Corporate Cultures: The Rites and Rituals of Corporate Life.* Harmondsworth: Penguin.

DfES (1989) *The Children Act 1999.* London: HMSO.

DfES (2003) *Every Child Matters.* http://www.everychildmatters.gov.uk

DfES (2004) *The Children Act 2004.* London: HMSO.

DfES (2005) *Common Care Skills and Knowledge for the Children's Workforce: Every Child Matters. Change for Children.* London: HMSO.

DfES (2006) *Working Together to Safeguard Children: A Guide to Inter-Agency Working to Safeguard and Promote the Welfare of Children. Every Child Matters: Change for Children.* London: HMSO.

Dimmock, B. (2002) *The Integration of Health and Social Care:* Unpublished paper, Milton Keynes School of Health and Social Welfare. Milton Keynes: The Open University.

DoH (1983) *The Mental Health Act 1983.* London: HMSO.

DoH (1990) *National Health Service Act 1990.* London: HMSO.

DoH (1997) *Community Care (Direct Payments) Act 1997.* London: HMSO.

DoH (1998) *Modernising Social Services.* London: HMSO.

DoH (1999) *National Service Framework for Older People.* London: HMSO.

DoH (1999) *Working Together to Safeguard Children.* London: HMSO.

DoH (2000) *A Quality Strategy for Social Care.* London: HMSO.

DoH (2000) *Care Standards Act 2000.* London: HMSO.

DoH (2001) *Fair Access to Care Services.* London: HMSO.

DoH (2001) *National Service Framework for Older People.* London: HMSO.

DoH (2001) *Valuing People.* London: HMSO.

DoH (2002) *Managing for Excellence in the NHS.* London: HMSO.

Dobson, S. and Stewart, R. (1993) What is Happening to Middle Management? In Mabey, C. and Mayon-White, B. *Managing Change.* 2nd edn. London: Paul Chapman Publishing.

Doyle, M., Claydon, T., Buchanan, D. (2000) Mixed Results, Lousy Process: the Management Experience of Organizational Change. *British Journal of Management* 11: 3, S59.

Drakeford, M. (2002) Poverty and the Social Services. In Bytheway, B. et al. (Eds.) *Understanding Care, Welfare and Community.* London: Routledge.

Druker, P.F. (1979) *Management.* London: Pan Books.

Dustin, D. (2000) Managers and Professionals: Another Perspective on Partnership. Managing *Community Care,* 8: 5.

Earl, M.J. and Hopwood, A.G. (1980) From Management Information to Information Management. In Lucas, H.C. et al. (Eds.) *The Information Systems Environment.* Amsterdam: North-Holland.

Fiedler, F.E. (1967) *A Theory of Leadership Effectiveness.* New York: McGraw-Hill.

Fisher, J. (1993) *Empirically Based Practice: The End of Ideology.* New York: Hamworth.

French, J.R.P. and Raven, B. (1959) The Basis of Social Power. In Cartwright, D. (Ed.) *Studies in Social Power.* Ann Arbor: University of Michigan.

General Social Care Council (2002a) *Standards and Values Expected of Employers.* London: GSCC.

General Social Care Council (2002b) *Code of Practice for Social Workers.* London: GSCC.

General Social Care Council (2005) *Specialist Standards and Requirements for Post-Qualifying Social Work Education and Training: Leadership and Management.* London: GSCC.

Giddens, A. (1998) *Is There a Third Way?* London: IEA Health and Welfare Unit.

Gill, R. (2006) *Theory and Practice of Leadership.* London: Sage.

Grant, R.M. (1995) *Cotemporary Strategy Analysis: Concepts, Techniques, Applications* 2nd Edn. Oxford: Blackwell.

Gray, A., Banks, S., Carpenter, J., Green, E. and May, T. (1999) *Professionalism and the Management of Local Authorities.* University of Durham: Centre for Public Management Research.

Handy, C. (1985) *Understanding Organisations.* Middlesex: Penguin.

Handy, C.B. (1993) *Understanding Organisations.* 4th edn. Middlesex: Penguin.

Harris, J. (1999) *Reclaiming Social Work: the Southport Papers.* Birmingham: Venture Press.

Hartley, J., Benington, J., Binns, P. (1997) Researching the Roles of Internal Change Agents in the Management of Organisational Change. *British Journal of Management.* 8: 61–73.

Hatton, C. et al. (1999) Organizational Culture and Staff Outcomes in Services for People with Intellectual Disabilities. *Journal of Intellectual Disability Research*, 43: 3, 206–18.

Have, S. et al. (2003) *Key Management Models.* Engelwood Cliffs, NJ: Prentice Hall.

Hayes, D. (2003) Recruitment is a Seller's Market. *Community Care*, 20.2.03.

Henderson, J. and Atkinson, D. (2003) *Managing Care in Context.* London: The Open University/Routledge and Kegan Paul.

Henwood, M. (2006) What's Driving Reform. *Community Care.* 21 July.

Hertzberg, F. (1992) One More Time: How do you Motivate Employees? In Gabarro, J.J. (Ed.) *Managing People and Organisations.* Boston, MA: Harvard Business School.

Herwood, M. (2005) What Drives Reform? *Community Care*, 21, July.

Higgins, J.M. and McAllaster, C. (2004) If You Want Strategic Change, Don't Forget to Change Your Cultural Artifacts. *Journal of Change Management*, 4: 1, 63–73.

Hofstede, G. and Hofstede, G.J. (2005) *Cultures and Organisations: Software of the Mind.* 2nd edn. New York: McGraw-Hill.

Hollis, F. (1992) *Social Casework.* New York: Randa House.

Hopson, B. and Adams, J. (1976) *Transition – Understanding and Managing Personal Change.* London: Martin Robinson.

Horner, N. (2003) *What is Social Work.* Exeter: Learning Matters.

Hunter, S. (2003) A Critical Analysis of Approaches to the Concept of Social Identity in Social Policy. *Critical Social Policy*, 23: 3, 322–44.

Irvine, R. et al. (2002) Interprofessionalism and Ethics: Consensus or Clash of Cultures. *Journal of Interprofessional Care*, 16: 199–210.

Jackson, A.C. and Donovan, F.H. (1999) *Managing to Survive: Managerial Practice in Not-for-Profit Organisations.* Buckingham: Open University Press.

Jacox, A. (1973) Professional Socialisation of Nurses. *Journal of the New York State Nurses' Association*, 4: 6–15.

James, A. (1992) Quality and its Social Construction by Managers in Care Service Organisations. In Kelly, D. and Warr, B. (Eds.) *Quality Counts: Achieving Quality in Social Care Services.* London: Whiting and Birch.

Johnson, G. (1992) Managing Strategic Change: Strategy, Culture and Action. *Long Range Planning*, 25: 1, 28–36.

Johnson, G. and Scholes, K. (1999) *Exploring Corporate Strategy.* 5th edn. Engelwood Cliffs, NJ: Prentice Hall.

Jordan, B. (1990) *Social Work and the Third Way.* London: Sage.

Jordan. B. (1997) Social Work and Society. In Davis, M. (Ed.) *Companion to Social Work.* Oxford: Blackwell.

Jordan, B. and Jordan, C. (2000) *Social Work and the Third Way: Social Policy as Tough Love.* London: Sage.

Kadushin, A. (1976) *Supervision in Social Work.* New York: Columbia University Press.

Kanter, R.M. (1983) *The Change Masters.* New York: Simon and Schuster.

Kemisar, R. (2002) Letter to the Editor. *Harvard Business Review.* (July) 119–20.

Komisar, R. (2002) Letters to the Editor: Reawakening Your Passion for Work. *Harvard Business Review.* 80: 7, 119–121.

Kotter, J.P. (1990) *A Force for Change: Now Leadership Differs from Management.* New York: Free Press.

LaFontaine, J. (1985) *Initiaation: Ritual, Drama and Secret Knowledge Across the World.* Harmondsworth: Penguin Books.

Laming, Lord. H. (2003) *The Victoria Climbiè Inquiry.* London: HMSO.

Lapsley, I. and Pong, G. (2000) Modernisation Versus Problematization: Value for Money Audit in Public Services. *The European Accounting Review*, 9: 541–6.

Le Grand, J. (1990) *Quasi Markets and Social Policy.* School of Advanced Urban Studies, Bristol University.

Leat, D. and Perkins, D. (1998) Juggling and Dealing: the Creative Work of Care Package Purchasing. *Social Policy and Administration*, 32: 2.

Leithwood, K., Jantzi, D. and Steinbach, R. (2000) *Changing Leadership for Changing Times.* Buckingham: The Open University Press.

Lewin, K. (1951) *Field Theory in Social Science.* New York: McGraw-Hill.

Ling, T. (2000) Unpacking Partnership in Health Care. In Clarke, J., Gerwitz, S. and McLoughlin, E.W. (2000) *New Managerialism, New Welfare?* Milton Keynes: Sage.

Lishman, J. (1994) *Communication in Social Work* Basingstoke: McMillan/BASW.

Locke, E. and Henne, D. (1986) *Work Motivation Theories.* In Cooper, C.L. and Robertson, I.T. (Eds.) *International Review of Industrial and Organisational Psychology.* New York: John Wiley and Sons.

Loney, M., Bocock, R., Clarke, J., Cochrane, A., Graham, P. and Wilson, M. (1991) *The State of the Market: Politics and Welfare in Contemporary Britain.* 2nd edn. London: Sage.

Lupton, T. (1971) *Management and the Social Sciences.* Middlesex: Penguin Books.

Mabey, C. and Mayon-White, B. (1993) *Managing Change.* 2nd edn. London: Paul Chapman Publishing.

Management Standards Centre (2004) *National Occupational Standards for Management and Leadership.* Management Standards Centre. http://www.msc.managers.org.uk

Martin, V. and Henderson, E. (2001) *Managing in Health and Social Care.* London: The Open University.

Maslow, A.H. (1970) *Motivation and Personality.* New York: Harper and Row.

Mendelow, A. (1991) Proceedings of 2nd International Conference on Information Systems, Cambridge MA. In Johnson, G. and Scholes, K. (2001) *Exploring Public Sector Strategy.* Englewood Cliffs, NJ: Prentice Hall.

Middlehurst, R. (1993) *Leading.* Buckingham: Open University Press.

Middleton, L. (1997) *The Art of Assessment.* Birmingham: Venture Press.

Miller, R. (2002) Motivating and Managing Knowledge Workers: Blending Strategy and Culture in Knowledge Organisations. *Knowledge Management Review*, 5: 1, 16–20.

Mintzberg, H. (1981) Organisations Design: Fashion or Fit? January/February, 106–16.

Molyneux, J. (2001) Interprofessional Team Working: What Makes Teams Work Well. *Journal of Interprofessional Care.* 15: 1.

Morita, A. (1986) *Akio Morita and SONY Made in Japan.* London: Fontana.

Mulgan, G. and Albury, D. (2003) *Innovation in the Public Sector.* At http://www.strategy.gov.uk/output/page4627.asp

Mullins, L.J. (1993) *Management and Organisational Behaviour.* London: Pitman.

Mullins, L.J. (2002) *Management and Organisational Behaviour.* Engelwood Cliffs, NJ: Prentice Hall.

Munroe, E. (2004) The Impact of Audit on Social Work Practice. *Journal of Social Work*, 34: 8, 1075–95.

Munroe-Faure, L. and Munroe-Faure, M. (1992) *Implementing Total Quality Management.* London: Pitman.

Murphy, M.A. (1988) *Decision Making in Paediatric Nursing.* Decker Publishing.

Naylor, J. (1999) *Management.* London: Pitman.

Nohria, N. and Eccles, R. (1992) Face to Face: Making Organisations Work. In Nohria, N. and Eccles, R. (Eds.) *Networks and Organisations: Structure, Form and Action.* Boston: Harvard Business School Press.

O'Connor, I. et al. (2006) *Social Work and Social Care Practice.* Milton Keynes: Sage.

O'Sullivan, T. (1999) *Decision Making in Social Work.* Basingstoke: Macmillan.

Øvretveit, J. (1997) *Interprofessional Working in Health and Social Care.* Basingstoke: Macmillan.

Parsloe, P. and Stevenson, O. (1978) *Social Services Teams; The Practitioner View.* London: DHSS.

Payne, M. (2006) Don't Live in Fear. *Professional Social Work.* June.

Payne, M. (2006) *Social Work: Themes, Issues and Critical Debates*, Basingstoke: Palgrave.

Payne, M. (2006) *What is Professional Social Work?* London: BASW/Policy Press.

Payne, M. (2006c) *What is Professional Social Work?* Bristol: Policy Press.

Peck, E., Gulliver, P. and Towell, D. (2002) Governance of Partnership in Health and Social Services: The Experience in Somerset. *Health and Social Care in the Community.* 10: 5, 331–8.

Performance and Innovation Unit (2001) *Strengthening Leadership in the Public Sector: A Research Study by the PIU.* London: The Cabinet Office.

Peters, T. and Waterman, R. (1980) Structure is not Organisation. In Quinn, J.B. and Mintzberg, H. (Eds.) *The Strategy Process.* Englewood Cliffs, NJ: Prentice Hall.

Pinnock, M. and Garnett, L. (2002) Needs Led or Needs Must: The Use of Needs-Based Information in Planning Children's Services. In Ward, H. and Rose, W. (Eds.) *Approaches to Needs Assessment in Children's Services.* London: Jessica Kingsley.

Platt, D. (2001) *The Children Act Now: Messages from Research.* London: Social Services Inspectorate.

Powell, F. (1999) *The Politics of Social Work.* London: Sage.

Prasad, R. (2001) Crisis in the Recruitment and Retention of Care Workers. *Society Guardian.*

Prime Minister's Strategy Unit (1999) *The Future and How to Think About It.* http://www.strategy.gov.uk

Prime Minister's Strategy Unit (2001) *Strengthening Leadership in the Public Sector: A research study by PIU.* London: The Cabinet Office.

Quality Assurance Agency (2000) *Social Policy and Administration and Social Work.* London: Quality Assurance Agency.

Quinney, A. (2006) *Collaborative Social Work Practice.* Exeter: Learning Matters.

Qureshi, H. (1998) Outcomes in Local Authorities. In Balloch, S. (Ed.) *Outcomes in Social Care: A Question of Quality?* London: NISW.

Rajan, A. (2000) Meaning of Management. *Professional Manager.* March 2000. p. 33.

Rogers, T. (2004) Managing in the Interprofessional Environment: A Theory of Action Perspective. *Journal of Interprofessional Care,* 18: 3, 239–61.

Rumelt, R. (1995) *Inerta and Transformation.* Fontainebleau, France: Insead.

Rummery (2002) *Working Together: Primary Care Involvement in Commissioning Social Care Services.* London: DoH.

Sapey, B. (2002) Physical Disability. In Adams, R., Dominelli, L. and Payne, M. (Eds.) *Critical Practice in Social Work.* Basingstoke: Palgrave.

Scase, R. (2000) *Britain in 2010.* Oxford: Capstone Publishing.

Schein, E. (1985) *Organisational Culture and Leadership.* 2nd edn. San Fransisco, CA: Jossey-Bass.

Schon, D.A. (1983) *The Reflective Practitioner.* New York: Basic Books.

Schwartz, H. and Davis, S. (1981) Matching Corporate Culture and Business Strategy. *Organisational Dynamics,* Summer, pp. 30–48.

Senge, P. (1996) Leading Learning Organisations: the Bold, the Powerful, and the Invisible. In Hesselbein, M., Goldsmith, M. and Beckhard, R. (Eds.) *The Leader of the Future.* San Francisco: Jossey-Bass.

Simon, R.W. (1992) Parental Role Strains, Salience of Parental Identity and Gender Differences in Psychological Distress. *Journal of Health and Social Behaviour,* 33: 25–35.

Skills for Care/TOPPS Report (2006) *Leadership and Management: A Strategy for the Social Care Workforce.* England: TOPPS.

Smale, G. (1996) *Mapping Change and Innovation.* London: HMSO.

Smale, G. (1998) *Managing Change Through Innovation.* London: HMSO.

Social Care Institute of Excellence (2005) *Developing Social Care: the Current Position.* London: SCIE.

Social Trends (2005) http://www.statistics.gov.uk

Southon, G. and Braithwait, J. (1998) The End of Professionalism? *Social Science and Medicine,* 46: 23–8.

Statham, D. (1996) *The Future of Social and Personal Care: the Role of Social Services Organisations in the Public, Private and Voluntary Sectors.* London: National Institute of Social Work.

Stryker, S. (1968) Identity Salience and Role Performance: The Importance of Symbolic Interaction Theory for Family Research. *Journal of Marriage and the Family,* 30: 388–99.

Terry, D.J., Hogg, M.A. and White, K.M. (1999) The Theory of Planned Behaviour: Self Identity, Social Identity and Group Norms. *British Journal of Psychological Society,* 38: 225.

Thompson, N. (2003) *Promoting Equality: Challenging Discrimination and Oppression in the Human Services.* 2nd edn. Basingstoke: Palgrave.

Trapp, R. (1999) Blunder Boss. *The British Journal of Administrative Management.* July/August 12–16.

Tsui, M. (2005) Functions of Social Work Supervision in Hong Kong. *International Social Work*. 48: 4, 485–93.

Turner, B. (2000) Supervision and Mentoring in Child and Family Social Work: The Role of the First-Line Manager in the Implementation of the Post-Qualifying Framework. *Social Work Education*, 1: 19, 3.

Wadhams, C. (2006) *An Opportunity Waiting to Happen: Housing Associations as 'Community Anchors'*. London: Home Office Active Community Unit and Bolton Community Homes.

Ward, K. et al. (2001) Dilemmas in the Management of Temporary Work Agency Staff. *Human Resource Management Journal*, 11: 4, 3–21.

Warr, B. and Kelly, D. (1992) What is Meant by Quality in Social Care? In *Quality Counts: Achieving Quality in Social Care Services*. London: Whiting and Birch/SCA.

Watson, T.J. (1986) *Management Organisation and Employment Strategy*. London: Routledge and Kegan Paul.

Wesley, F. and Mintzberg, H. (1991) Visionary Leadership and Strategic Management. In Henry, J. and Walker, D. (Eds.) *Managing Innovation*. London: Sage.

Westhues, A., Lafrance, J. and Schmidt, G. (2001) A SWOT Analysis of Social Work Education in Canada. *Social Work Education*, 20: 1, 35–56.

Whittington, C. (2003) Collaboration and Partnership in Context. In Weinstein, J., Whittington, C. and Leiba, T. (Eds.) *Collaboration in Social Work Practice*. London: Jessica Kingsley.

Williams, F. and Popay, J. (1999) Balancing Polarities: Developing a New Framework for Welfare Research. In Williams, F., Popay, J. and Oakley, A. (Eds.) *Welfare Research: A Critical Review*. London: UCL.

Williams, I. and Young, J. (2003) Managing the Transient Workforce: Thinking, Knowledge Sharing and Transfer in the Social Services Arena. http://www.knowledgeboard.com

Winstanley, D.D., Sorabji, S. and Dawson, S. (1995) When the Pieces Don't Fit: A Stakeholder Power Matrix to Analyse Public Sector Restructuring. *Public Money and Management*, Apr–Jun, 19–26.

Wolstenholme, E. et al. (2006) *Balancing Supply and Demand in Health and Social Care Organisations*. http://www.symmetricsd.co.uk

Yukl, G. (1994) *Leadership in Organisations*. 3rd edn. Engelwood Cliffs, NJ: Prentice Hall.

Zaccaro, S.J. and Banks, D.J. (2001) Leadership, Vision and Organizational Effectiveness. In S.J. Zaccaro and R.J. Klimoski (Eds.) *The Nature of Organizational Leadership*. San Francisco, CA: Jossey-Bass.

Index